Favorite Poetry Lessons

by Paul B. Janeczko

SCHOLASTIC
PROFESSIONAL BOOKS

NEW YORK • TORONTO • LONDON • AUCKLAND • SYDNEY
MEXICO CITY • NEW DELHI • HONG KONG

❧ DEDICATION ❧

Dedicated with affection and gratitude to those teachers who understand the power of the written word and share that power with young writers.

❧ ACKNOWLEDGMENT ❧

This book would have been impossible without the generous spirit and wild imagination of the many young writers who were so willing to share their work with me. I thank them all.

Page 39, Four clerihews by E.C. Bentley. Reproduced with permission of Curtis Brown Ltd.
London on behalf of the Estate of E.C. Bentley © E.C. Bentley.

Page 42, "Useless Things" from *A Mouse in My Roof* by Richard Edwards. Copyright © 1988 by Richard Edwards.
Used by permission of Delacorte Press, a division of Bantam Doubleday Dell Publishing Group, Inc.

Page 59, "The Big Field" from *Baseball, Snakes, and Summer Squash: Poems About Growing Up* by Donald Graves.
Copyright © 1996 by Donald Graves. Used by permission of Boyds Mills Press.

Page 84, "Ten Little Likenesses" by X.J. Kennedy. Reprinted with the permission of Margaret K. McElderry Books, an imprint of Simon & Schuster Children's
Publishing Division from *The Kite That Braved Old Orchard Beach* by X.J. Kennedy. Text copyright © 1991 by X.J. Kennedy.

Page 81, "Scarecrow's Dream" by Nina Nyhart. From *Openers*, Alice James Books. Rerpinted by permission of Nina Nyart.

Page 68, "A History of the Pets" from *Stopping by Home*, copyright © 1988 by David Huddle. Reprinted by permission of David Huddle.

Page 70, "How to Make a Snow Angel" from *Water Planet* by Ralph Fletcher. Copyright © 1991 by Ralph Fletcher.
All rights reserved. Reprinted by permission of Marian Reiner.

Page 80, "Letter to a Friend" from *Sam's Place* in *Something New Begins* by Lilian Moore. Copyright © 1967, 1969, 1972, 1975, 1980, 1982 by Lilian Moore.
Copyright renewed by Liliane Moore. Reprinted by permission of Marian Reiner.

Page 36, excerpt from *Opposites: Poems and Drawings* by Richard Wilbur.
Copyright © 1973 by Richard Wilbur, reprinted by permission of Harcourt Brace & Company.

Page 83, "Cow's Complaint" from *How Now, Brown Cow?*, copyright © 1994 by Alice Schertle,
reprinted by permission of Harcourt Brace & Company.

Page 74, "Old Farm in Northern Michigan" from *Blue Like the Heavens: New and Selected Poems* by Gary Glidner, copyright © 1984.
Reprinted by permission of the University of Pittsburgh Press.

Cover design by Jaime Lucero
Interior design by Solutions by Design, Inc.

Table of Contents

Confessions of a Poetry Fanatic

I didn't set out to be a poet. I started out as a kid in New Jersey who had two major goals in life: (1) to survive another year of delivering newspapers without being attacked by Ike, the one-eyed crazy cur that lurked in the forsythia bushes at the top of the hill; and (2) to become more than a weak-hitting, third-string catcher on our sorry Little League team. I failed at both.

Had I announced at the dinner table, "Mom, Dad, I've decided to be a poet," my parents—especially my mother—would have been thrilled. In truth, they would have been thrilled that I'd decided to be *anything* other than the top-40 disk jockey or bullpen catcher I constantly talked about becoming in junior high.

Back then, poetry meant no more to me than George Washington's wooden teeth, gerunds, or the chief exports of the Belgian Congo. I only read poetry when I had to. Instead, I read baseball magazines, the daily sports page, and baseball cards old and new. I was captivated by those small color pictures of men wearing five o'clock shadows and baggy flannel pants. I was seduced by the sweet poetry of their nicknames: Whale, Runt, Blimp, and Porty. Boots, Bloop, Hoot, and Scooter. And Suitcase Bob, Jungle Jim, Sudden Sam.

Although I never caught a pitch beyond the Little League level or bantered between tunes over the radio waves, years later, by some ironic twist of fate, I found myself teaching high school and reading poetry instead of baseball cards. Somehow I had become a poetry fanatic. I read poetry the way people watch soap operas, work on cars, or follow the Red Sox: irrationally, compulsively, endlessly. It is this delicious fanaticism that I want your students to feel.

I became a writer of poetry too. I consider myself lucky, given my astounding lack of interest and effort in school and in the poetry I was expected to read. But kids today don't have to rely on luck to become readers and writers of poetry because of teachers like you, who share poetry with them in ways that are joyous, not arduous. I hope that this book will be one of many tools you will use to put kids and poetry together. I hope that the exercises and activities in this book will show what Robert Francis meant when he said, "One word cannot strike sparks from itself; it takes at least two for that. It takes two words lying side by side on the page to breed wonders."

Getting Started

When I was in grammar school, we read ponderous verse from thick volumes with names like *Come Hither!* and *Poet's Gold*. The poems had no connection to life as I and my friends knew it. Thankfully, that has changed. Middle-school classrooms are filled with books, many of them the work of poets like Valerie Worth and Jack Prelutsky, Jeff Moss and Karla Kuskin. And, not surprisingly, kids enjoy poetry much more than they did in the days when I was forced to memorize "Trees" by Joyce Kilmer.

The Poetry-Friendly Classroom

The best way to create a verse-rich learning environment is to become a poetry reader. If you are a true poetry reader, your classroom will reflect that. You will make poetry part of the entire curriculum instead of saving it for a gigantic poetry unit in April. If you are a true poetry reader, you will find many poems to share with your kids. Read an apple poem in the fall, a sports poem when your team is going into the finals, a poem about loss when someone in your community dies, a poem about living anytime. The best teachers in the schools I visit link poetry to the real world. They share the poems that connect with something that happened at school or in the world. These are the poems that hit the mark.

Read poetry aloud to your students. We need not be Al Pacino or Glenn Close to read to a class. Kids appreciate a sincere, expressive reader. You can, by the way, practice reading poems aloud under almost any circumstances: softly to a sleeping baby, to an attentive hound, to a spouse. Reading aloud lets us hear the music of the words, something we frequently miss when we read silently. There should be no tests or reports, no strings attached when we read poems aloud to a class: just the joy of hearing our language used at its best.

WRITE POEMS YOURSELF

Try to work along with the kids on poetry-writing assignments. This gives you a better sense of what your students are going through, and you can show them how you work through the writing process. Nothing fosters a poetry-friendly classroom more than when the teacher and the students work on the same poetry explorations.

TAKE RISKS

Kids need to know that it's okay to try something new, even though they may fail at first. Many young writers—and not-so-young writers as well—continue doing something they're good at, like writing haiku or limericks, rather than trying something risky, like free verse. But if we want our kids to grow as writers, we need to encourage them to go toward something different, and we have to cheer their efforts when they venture into uncharted waters.

START A POETRY LIBRARY

One of the simplest ways to make your classroom poetry-friendly is to fill it with poetry books and let the kids have at them. Give them some time to browse through the books, looking for poems they like. You might even ask some students to read newly discovered poems to the class, or invite them to consider the connection between a poem and the art that appears with it. Later, they may wish to illustrate their own poems or those of classmates.

> ### ❧ IN THE POET'S WORDS... ❧
>
> "Above all, poetry is intended for the ear. It must be felt to be understood, and before it can be felt it must be heard. Poets listen for their poems, and we, as readers, must listen in turn. If we listen hard enough, who knows?—we too may break into dance, perhaps for grief, perhaps for joy."
>
> —Stanley Kunitz

MAKE CONNECTIONS

Link poetry to other reading—fiction and nonfiction—that the class is doing. There are countless poems that can enrich your social studies or science lessons. Kids can read poems about the Holocaust after reading *The Diary of Anne Frank*. Or they can select an appropriate poem from Lee Bennett Hopkins' anthology, *Hand in Hand: An American History Through Poetry*. Students can also write poems in other subject areas. Throughout this book I've made suggestions for how to apply various forms of poetry across the curriculum.

When I was in school, it seemed that poetry was meant to puzzle, to intimidate and infuriate me and my friends. We need to show young readers and writers that poetry can comfort, advise, recall, describe, narrate, mourn, and warn. It can mesmerize, mock, and mimic. It can celebrate, provoke, praise, and remember. Above all, young readers need to see that poetry sings of human experiences. And they *will* see this when exciting poetry plays an integral part in your classroom.

Activities for Warming Up With Words

I want young writers to understand that poetry is made up of words that have sound, meaning, and feeling. They may say they know all this, but I'm not always convinced that they realize what "this" means. So I usually begin our poetry-writing time with an exercise that gives them a chance to literally play with words.

THE WORD BOX

For this activity, which poets have used for years, fill a small box with slips of paper on which are printed evocative words and phrases. (I have used a coffee can to hold my words. Then I call it…well, I call it the Word Can.) Introduce the box to the class by shaking it so that the kids can hear the papers rattling around. When I do this with a class, they have no idea what's inside. "Rice?" one kid suggests. "Seeds? Pencil points? Rust?" other students offer. "All good guesses," I tell them, "but no, this is the world-famous Word Box." They look at each other, puzzled. "You've heard of it, of course," I say. "No? Well, it's a good thing I brought it." By now, the kids are begging me to open it. I carefully lift the lid and let the kids peer over the edge of the box at the tangle of words. The kids are hooked.

"I'm going to give each of you a sprinkle of words," I say, as I make my way around the room giving each kid a small pile of words. "And what I want you to do is see what combinations you can make. Do *not* try to write a poem with your words. Do *not* use all the words to make one long sentence. Play with the words. Make interesting combinations. Put together some words that sound nice, or scary. Create combinations that make you happy or that make you sad. Have fun with the meaning of the words, the sounds of the words. Surprise yourself!"

As the kids begin to work with their words, I prowl around the room answering questions. Yes, you can add your own words. These are starter words. Yes, you can change the endings of words, making verbs past tense or nouns plural, for example. Before long, kids are asking if they can read a phrase out loud. Let it rip, I tell them. Others join in. As kids read their word combinations to their classmates, we hear some wonderful, wacky, often surreal, combinations.

After they've had time to read aloud to the class, I tell the kids to write down in their notebooks the keepers—any combinations they especially liked. I want them to keep their best phrases, because a poem might be lurking there. Later, when they're trying to find something to write about, I suggest that they look over their lists. A phrase might make a good opening line or title for a poem, or it may simply give them a nudge to explore new territory. Kids delight in saving such surreal goodies as:

> a flock of flying fish grave breath
> Mama said that day there were snapdragons in the dark
> Screaming penguins had a blast eating inside the factory
> alien snowflakes
> sunflower breath
> her teeth and acorns
> My sticky sister has very crafty nightmares
> Maybe a fish blew his nose, but what if he didn't?

Some of the words I used when I tried the Word Box for the first time came from *Beyond Words: Writing Poems With Children*, a wonderful book by Elizabeth McKim and Judith W. Steinbergh. I borrowed their most interesting words—words like *yelped, blast, ouch,* and *not too long ago*—and added my own. But a good Word Box is like the starter that a baker uses when making sourdough—it helps the ideas for poems to ferment. And it's not meant to be a static collection. Kids can take out a word they're tired of, trade words, add words.

A CLASS WORD BOOK

I keep available a notebook with "Young Poets' Word Book" emblazoned across its cover. I let the kids know that this Word Book is theirs. It is a place for them to write any word they find interesting, silly, sad. Words they want share with the class. Words like *ironic, lump, creepy, bossy, bashing-lashing-dashing, pouncing*. From time to time, I go through the book searching for good words to add to the Word Box (and, yes, blacking out the occasional inappropriate word). I urge students to look through the book whenever they have a spare minute. They may very well find a word that they want to add to one of their lists.

PERSONAL WORD LISTS

Invite students to set aside ten or so pages in their writing journals for a running Word List. These lists may be haphazard when kids first begin collecting, but as they add more words and attune their ears to the sounds and nuances of meaning, they should begin to organize their words into categories. For example, they might have a list of words that sound funny to them or ones that are jarring to their ears: musical words like *feather, balloon, smooth,* and *willow*; "clang" words like *freckles, snake, kick,* and *grab*; color words like *chartreuse, mossy, schoolbus yellow*; night words—*inky, starry, slumber, hush*; words that have texture; soft words; words they associate with home; happy words like *ointment*—it's hard to say *ointment* without smiling. They may be as surprised by their categories as they are by the words they've collected.

or post-it

10

INVENTED WORDS

Students can make up words, as we all did before we learned to speak but simply liked to hear sounds coming from our mouths. You could get your writers into the spirit of making up words by asking them to come up with definitions that seem to fit the words. Maybe *krondorf* means "the small threaded part that screws onto the top of a lamp." Or *mip* might mean "a noise a cat frequently makes in its sleep." Who knows? Have fun!

THESAURUS TREASURE TROVE

Make sure students' lists includes words that appeal to all the senses. Let the kids look through a thesaurus. Ask them to make a list of other words for *red* (*scarlet, ruby, vermilion, russet, cherry, auburn, titian*) or purple (*lilac, lavender, mauve, orchid, plum, violet*).

WORDS OF THE WORLD

How about having students make a list of names from an atlas? Towns like Pomoho, Yolo, Clute, and Clackamas are packed with poetic sound. They could compile a list of rivers: Darling, Limpopo, Salween, and Ob. Or mountains: Rosa, Musala, Apo, Misti, Pissis, and Illimani. Let kids have fun rolling these words around in their mouths! Bring in some field guides for interesting words related to birds, insects, rocks, mushrooms, and shells.

DICTIONARY GAME

One way to get kids thinking about real words is to let them play the Dictionary Game. You know the one: Someone in the group looks through the dictionary until she finds an unfamiliar word. When she says the word, everyone else makes up a definition of it and writes it on a slip of paper. The one who looked up the word copies the real definition on a slip of paper and adds it to the others. Then she reads aloud all the definitions and the others guess which is the correct definition. The person who pens the most convincing definition scores a point.

🌿 IN THE POET'S WORDS... 🌿

"The great thing about collecting words is that they're free; you can borrow them, trade them in or toss them out.... Words are lightweight, unbreakable, portable, and they're everywhere. You can even make them up."

—Susan Goldsmith Wooldridge

RHYMING DICTIONARY

Many young writers that I meet don't know that such a book exists, so when I show them one, they're amazed at what they behold. As they browse through it, a wave of giggles and guffaws often erupts as students discover the music of rhyme. They delight, for instance, in rhymes for *blues: boos, bruise, chews, choose, clues, cruise, dues, fuse, glues, hues, lose, mews, moos, muse, news, ooze, ruse, shoes, snooze, stews.* And rhymes for *bloom: boom, broom, doom, fume, gloom, groom, loom, plume, room, tomb, whom, womb, zoom.*

How to Get "Inspired"

Young writers always ask me where I get ideas for my poems. They're often surprised when I tell them that ideas for poems are all around them—they just need to look and listen. And they need to save their ideas. I encourage kids to keep a small notebook for jotting down things they see and hear and ideas that come to mind from who-knows-where. "Oh, I can write down my ideas when I get home," they assure me. Maybe, but many of them don't, because they're sidetracked by chores at home, play, homework, or television, and they simply forget to write them down.

USE MEMORIES

Students will also get ideas for poems from their memories. Once again, however, they need to capture those memories on paper. Maybe a few words or sentences will be enough to allow them to fill in the details at a later time. For example, one morning I woke cold and noticed my wife had pulled the covers away from me. I was immediately reminded of how, when I was a kid, my younger brother had done the same thing to me. That memory was telling me to pay attention to it, which I did, eventually writing this poem:

BLANKET HOG

When my brother
hogs the blanket,
the only thing to do
is yank it.

When your students are gathering ideas, it's important that they realize that there is never a guarantee that they will get a poem out of one particular inspiration. At the same time, they also need to understand that there is no correct subject to write a poem about, nor is there a correct way to write a poem about a specific idea. Thumb through any good anthology, and you'll see how poets have written poems in different styles at different times about the same subject.

12

TAKE AN OBSERVATION STROLL

To get students started observing and taking notes, take your class on an Observation Walk through the school, around the grounds, or, best of all, through the neighborhood. When I did this with a class, I made sure they saw me jotting in my notebook. Back in the room, I shared my notes with the kids and told them of a couple of ideas I had gotten from my observations. Then I asked them if they had any thoughts about how I might deal with some of my notes. As usual, I was pleasantly surprised with their suggestions.

After we had talked at length about my observations, I asked my students if any of them wanted to share an observation or two. After some silence and nervous glancing about the room, one hand rose tentatively. The rest was a snap. Getting that first young writer to share is often like getting the first pickle from the pickle jar. After that, the rest come easily.

It's a good idea to check in with the kids regularly to see what they've noticed about the world around them. It also lets them know that you believe that being an active observer is part of being a good writer. Setting aside time when kids can share their notes and discuss ways that a particular subject can be developed in a poem also pays dividends. Young poets need to know that good poetry explodes with possibilities.

PACK A POETRY SUITCASE

I frequently bring to class a small overnight suitcase filled with…well, it's filled with stuff: crazy stuff, like a gaudy paper birthday hat and a brass gizmo from my recently repaired furnace; cute stuff, like a stuffed animal and a picture of a fluffy puppy; and everyday stuff, like one black glove and a pair of sunglasses. As is true of the Word Book, the Poetry Suitcase is a place where students can look for ideas when they have a minute between poems or when they're waiting for a conference. Most often, when students avail themselves of this resource, they do not write about a specific object. Rather, the items in the suitcase frequently trigger a memory, and *that's* where their poems come from. And, of course, I always accept donations for the suitcase.

A Look at the Writing Process

Just as there is no right way to get topics for a poem, there is no right writing process. Generally, though, a good piece of writing goes through a number of stages before it's complete: brainstorming, drafting, editing, revising, publishing. I tell young writers that when I write poems, I usually go through the same steps that they do. To be sure, it takes me longer, and a couple of the steps are more intense, especially editing and revising, but the *process* is the same.

BRAINSTORMING

Let me use "Prince of the Dump," a poem in my collection, *Stardust   otel*, to illustrate the process.

Since the poem is based on a character, I wanted to make the subject interesting, because if I can create an interesting character, he or she will do interesting things, and that will engage readers. I began by writing the character's name at the top of a legal sheet of paper. Then I simply wrote down whatever came into my mind about this character. It was important for me not to censor myself by listening to my inner critic, who is great at whispering (sometimes yelling) things like, "What a lame idea!" or "That will never work!" or "That is the stupidest thing I have ever seen!" At this point in the process, there are no bad ideas. All I was doing was trying to look at some of the possibilities for this character.

Slowly, I add things to my sheet, answering questions like, Where did he come from? What does he look like? Sound like? What is his secret? Does he have a distinctive way of walking, talking, living? To get to know some basic information about my characters, I have, on occasion, filled out an actual job application from my local supermarket for each of them. Of course, I'm not going to use all that information in a poem—it doesn't belong—but that information helps me get to know the character better.

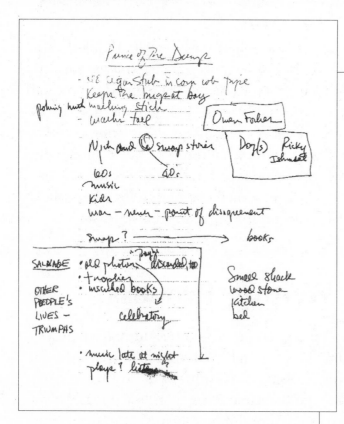

My first draft—thank goodness first drafts don't have to be neat.

14

DRAFTING

When I sensed that I had enough information, I started drafting the poem, building it word by word, phrase by phrase. I paused frequently to read parts aloud. I asked myself which word sounded better; I tinkered; I moved words around; I played with line breaks. Parts of the poem came and went, until I thought the draft was finished.

A later draft—even though I've moved the poem to the computer, I'm still playing around with lanuage.

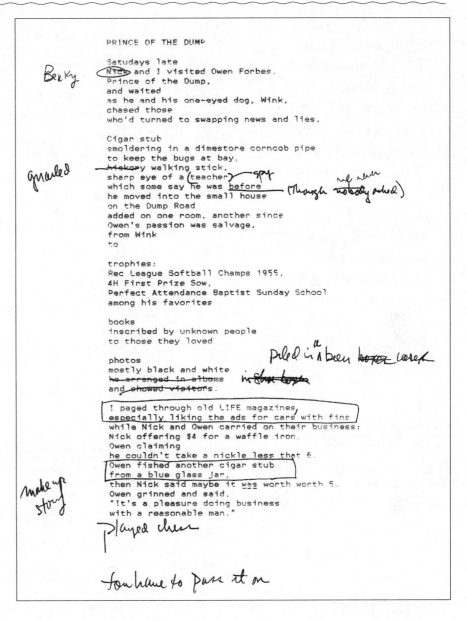

RESTING

When I think I've done as much with the draft as I can, I put it in a folder for a few weeks or a few months to let it rest. This is an important part of the writing process, but we normally give kids only a few days to complete a writing assignment. However, letting the poem rest out of sight gives me the time to look at it fresh and see how it affects me. If it affects me as it did when I put it in the folder, I feel that I may very well be onto something.

REWRITING

Now comes the hard part—rewriting. It's an often odious task that not many writers I know look forward to, but if a piece of writing has any chance of being good, a writer, young or old, must rewrite. And so I began to tinker, to tear out unnecessary words, to play with the length of lines, to read parts aloud to better hear the music of the words. Thanks to my marvelous computer, I easily made changes and printed out revised versions until I got the poem that I thought was the best I could make it.

At this point in the process, there are fewer changes because the poem is becoming sharper.

```
PRINCE OF THE DUMP

Saturdays late
Becky and I visited Owen Forbes,
Prince of the Dump,
and waited
as he and his one-eyed dog, Wink,
chased those
who'd stopped to swap news and lies.

Cigar but,
smoldering in a dimestore corncob pipe
to keep the bugs at bay,
gnarled walking stick,
shape eye of a spy,
which some said he was before
though we never asked)          no one
before he moved into the small house
on the Dump Road,
added on one room, another, since
Owen's passion was salvage,
from Wink,
left to die in a trash bag,
to

trophies:
Rec League Softball Champs 1985,
4H First Prize Sow,
Perfect Attendance Baptist Sunday School
among his favories;

books
inscribed by unknown people
to those they loved;

photos
mostly black and white
Almost Stacked piled in a beer case, but one Theme

I paged through old LIFE magazines,
especially liking the ads for cars with fins;
Owen fished another cigar stub
from a blue glass jar;
Becky pawed through the photos
until she found one she wanted:
smiling mother, father, sad-eyed daughter
forever happy.
```

TINKERING

But even then, "Prince of the Dump" wasn't really finished. I looked at it many times before I sent it out to my agent, changing a word here, punctuation there. Someone once said a poem is never finished. It is released. But it should only be released when we have done all we can to make it touch the heart.

Prince of the Dump

Saturdays late
Owen Forbes
Prince of the Dump,
and his one-eyed dog, Wink,
chased those
who'd stopped to swap news and lies.

Cigar butt
smoldering in Woolworth corncob pipe
to keep the bugs at bay,
gnarled walking stick,
sharp eye of a spy,
which some said he was
(though we never asked)
before he moved into the small house
on the Dump Road,
added one room, another
since Owen's passion was salvage,
from Wink,
left to die in a trash bag,
to
trophies
Rec League Softball Champs 1985
4-H First Prize Sow
Perfect Attendance Baptist
    Sunday School
among his favorites;

books
inscribed by unknown people
to those they loved;
photos
mostly black-and-white
stacked in a beer case,
except the one
he slid into a silver frame:
smiling mother, father,
   sweet-faced girl
forever happy.

                —Paul B. Janeczko

FAVORITE POETRY LESSONS
Scholastic Professional Books, 1998

How to Use This Book

Anyway you want.

Having said that, let me explain how the book is set up. The poetry-writing activities and suggestions are divided into two major sections: Writing Poems That Rhyme and Writing Free Verse. I tried to move from simpler forms and concepts to more sophisticated ones. However, just like a diet of snails or grapefruit can become tiresome and unappealing, so it is with writing poetry. Although the rhyming poems and the free-verse poems are in separate sections, I would never suggest that my way of organizing the material in this book is *the* way to teach poetry writing. It is one way that has worked for me. True, some forms seem to complement each other, like the synonym, opposite, and clerihew. Nonetheless, you shouldn't hesitate to mix the rhyming with the free-verse poems if you think that will work better for you. Choose the poems that will engage your kids. Modify the activities in a way that will best enable you to make poetry an integral part your teaching.

I encourage you to personalize this book in every way that will help it serve you and your students better. Use the margins and note pages in the back of the book to jot down ideas, poems, and other inspirations that may come to you as you read the poems and exercises. If you're interested in sharing with me poems you use, modifications you make, or comments you have, feel free to send them my way in care of Scholastic Professional Books. I'd love to hear from you.

One last word about this book. It contains material that I've used successfully with students in grades 4–8 in schools in this country and overseas. However, don't be shy about adjusting an assignment designed for younger kids to make it suitable for your older students. The books that I mention throughout contain a riches of poems for readers of all ages, so do some browsing of your own to find the poems that are right for your kids.

Worth Reading

The following resources provide more suggestions for creating a poetry-friendly class.

Beyond Words: Writing Poems With Children by Elizabeth McKim and Judith Wolinsky Steinbergh (second edition) is a gold mine of ideas. You can order it from Talking Stone Press, 99 Evans Road, Brookline, MA 02146.

For the Good of the Earth and Sun by Georgia Heard (Heinemann, 1989) and *Explore Poetry* by Donald H. Graves (Heinemann, 1992) both include solid, practical suggestions that will engage young writers and convey an attitude toward teaching poetry that is remarkable.

poemcrazy by Susan Goldsmith Wooldridge (Random House, 1997) is about "freeing your life with words." Although this book is intended for more advanced writers, a number of the exercises—especially some of her word-collecting activities—could be used with young writers. But read it for yourself if you think there's a poet dying to bust out of you.

Reading and Writing Poetry: A Guide for Teachers by Judith Wolinsky Steinbergh (Scholastic Professional Books) is packed with activities for kids and teachers in grades K–4.

Teaching Poetry: Yes You Can! by Jacqueline Sweeney (Scholastic Professional Books) covers many of the bases of getting kids in grades 4–8 to write poetry—for example, strong verbs, imagery, and structure.

Writing Poems That Rhyme

Kids love to write rhyming poems. They may complain about the "rules," but it's these very rules that let them feel safe when they write. When they write rhyming poems, they know that the line is going to end at the rhyme, and that gives them comfort. Plus they love the rhythm rhyming poems afford.

Many young writers, however, get into trouble when they try to write a serious poem with end rhyme. That happens because young people do not always have the vocabulary to write about a serious subject in a poem that rhymes. Consequently, their poems frequently sound stilted and stiff. The rhyme sounds forced. Let me use one of my poems to illustrate what I mean:

ODD COUPLE

> Loud and flashy, my Aunt Stella
> Likes to wink at every fella.
> Absent minded, Uncle Francis
> Can't remember where his pants is.

Now, *Francis* and *pants is* is a delightful rhyme, but only in the context of a nonsense poem. I would never attempt that sort of outrageous rhyme about a series subject, like crime or divorce. So I try to let young writers work with many different forms of mostly light rhyming poems in which they can get away with silly rhymes that allow them to exercise their poetic license.

❧ IN THE POET'S WORDS... ❧

"I really do think of form as a safe place…. The form of a poem delivers what it promises. There are boundaries, and consequently you're free. [Writing free verse is] much, much more difficult. The decision-making interferes with the flow of my art."

— Molly Peacock

Over time, I've developed a method of approaching poetry writing in the classroom. Although there is always room for variation, I usually follow these steps:

1 READ POEMS. Whenever I introduce a new form of rhyming poetry, like a synonym poem, I always give each student a sheet of model poems. They appreciate having a number of examples, and they can underline features and jot down notes that will help them draft their poems. When possible, I mix poems written by students with poems written by professional adult poets. I want kids to read the best possible examples of the type of poem I'm inviting them to write, but at the same time, I don't want them to feel intimidated reading only the work of established poets. Reading powerful poems written by their peers boosts students' confidence and often evokes an if-she-can-do-it-I-can-do-it response.

2 DISCUSS POEMS. I ask students to read the model poems to themselves and think about what they notice. For example, what things might make a synonym poem? What do the poems have in common? I write students' responses on the board. I encourage them to look carefully at the poems, to not reject an idea because it seems too insignificant to mention. They might feel, for example, that it's not important to mention that each synonym poem is two lines long or that many of them are humorous.

3 WRITE A CLASS POEM FIRST. After adding to the list any elements that might have escaped my students' notice, we write a class poem. My role is to guide students and write their responses on the board. This step—writing a class poem— is crucial because it gives us all a chance to witness the writing process in action. When we have finished our poem, we will have moved from brainstorming to a "published" piece—one written on the board. Along the way, if I'm lucky, the students will haggle about this line or that word and argue about which line completes the poem best. They will, in short, be making the kinds of decisions all writers make.

4 HAVE CHILDREN WRITE ON THEIR OWN. Now students are ready to write their own poems. That's my cue to assume my role as cheerleader, encouraging kids to take a chance and experiment with their poem's subject and its language. I circulate among students, and when I find someone who has written a line or two that would serve as a good example, I read it aloud (after getting the writer's permission). And so the class goes for perhaps the next 20 minutes or so, the kids writing and me coaching.

I try to give students time to write their poems with care, so I will allow them an additional class period to work on them and to confer with me and their peers. When students have had time to finish the assignment, which might be to write

FAVORITE POETRY LESSONS
Scholastic Professional Books, 1998

four synonym poems or 10 lines of opposites, I read their work carefully at home, looking for the best from each student. Often, some poems need more revision; others are finished.

5 SHARE POEMS. When I have the best poems—and I try to find at least one acceptable poem from each writer—I have them typed and copied, then distributed to the class in a booklet. The writing process is complete. We can all enjoy the fruits of our work by reading the poems silently. I also allow time for interested students to read their work aloud.

As you read the following poems and activities, try them out yourself. Get a feel for the poems and for how the activities work before you share them with your students. Enjoy!

❧ IN THE POET'S WORDS... ❧

"Working in rhyme, you don't absolutely control the direction your poem is heading in. At times, you yearn to say something, but the infernal rhymes won't let you. You're like someone crossing a river on stepping-stones, obliged to walk where the stones permit. You struggle to keep your balance, while at the same time trying to go where you want to go. Often, in writing a rhyming poem, you end up somewhere you didn't expect."

—X. J. Kennedy

❧ I Made a Mistake ❧

I went to the bathroom to brush my hair,
I made a mistake…and brushed a bear.

I went to the kitchen to bake a pie,
I made a mistake…and baked a fly.

I went through my drawers to find a blouse,
I made a mistake…and found a mouse.

I went to the well to make a wish,
I made a mistake and…kissed a fish.

I went to the laundry to wash my socks,
I made a mistake…and washed a fox.

I went to the store to buy a cake,
I made a mistake…and bought a snake.

I went to the closet to put on my hat,
I made a mistake…and put on the cat.

I went next door to find my friend,
I made a mistake …and found THE END.

—a classic jump-rope rhyme

FAVORITE POETRY LESSONS
Scholastic Professional Books, 1998

❧ I Made a Mistake ❧

WRITING SIMPLE RHYMES

When I introduce writing rhyming poems to a class, I start with simple rhymes and move on to longer or more sophisticated ones. "I Made a Mistake," a traditional jump rope rhyme, is a good one to use with students who do not yet have a lot of poetry-writing experience.

READ THE POEM

After I hand out copies of the poem, I ask for a volunteer to read it aloud. It also makes for good choral reading, with two students reading alternate couplets. Since this is a jump rope rhyme, this poem provides a good example of rhythm.

DISCUSS THE POEM

Now we look at the poem. I ask students, "What do you notice? How has this poet structured the poem?" The students see that the poem is written in *couplets* (two lines of poetry that rhyme). They also see that it follows a pattern: The first line always begins with "I went"; the second begins with "I made a mistake…and…." Then we look further to see that, in the first line, the narrator goes somewhere to do something. In the second line the narrator makes a mistake and does something else.

Beyond the poem's pattern, I want students to notice the surprise in the second line—surprise that is in a sense set up by what happens in the first line. I encourage kids to have fun with this poem. Where can they go? Anywhere! To do what? Anything! And then—the surprise. What can happen that will get a chuckle from the reader? The possibilities are wide open, and I urge the young writers to use their imaginations and not to be afraid to try something wild.

WRITE COUPLETS

After we've written a couplet or two on the board, I turn the kids loose. Their job is to write one couplet that can become part of a class poem.

"What should we do when we finish a couplet?" a student often asks.

"Write another!" I implore. "Never stop writing when the ideas are coming fast and furious."

HAVE A READ AROUND

In a short time, everyone has written at least one couplet. We then have a Read Around, during which students read their couplets aloud. Although I prefer to have every student contribute to a class poem, I let them know that they always have the right to not read. They simply have to say "Pass" when it's their turn. No questions asked. No hard feelings. I make it a point, however, to visit with any student who continues to pass when it's his or her turn to see if there is a problem. It could be that the student feels he doesn't read well, in which case I will offer to read for him. Or, if the writer lacks confidence in what she's written, I do what I can to boost her confidence. Frequently, finding something in her work to praise and offering to read it aloud for her will do the trick.

By the time my students were finished with their couplets, they had written some wonderful rhymes. One class of fourth graders came up with the poem that appears on the next page.

FAVORITE POETRY LESSONS
Scholastic Professional Books, 1998

❧ I Went to... ❧

I went to the barn to put on a saddle,
I made a mistake…and sat on a paddle.

I went to the kitchen to cook a steak,
I made a mistake…and cooked a rake.

I went to the fair to go on a ride,
I made a mistake…and fell off the side.

I went to the store to buy some towels,
I made a mistake…and came home with an owl.

I went to the barn to feed the pig,
I made a mistake…and danced a jig.

I went to the mall to buy some shoes,
I made a mistake…and played the blues.

I went on a date to have some cake,
I made a mistake…and ate a plate.

I went to the store to buy a shirt,
I made a mistake…and fell in the dirt.

I went to my class to learn some math,
I made a mistake…and took a bath.

I went to Europe to visit Rome,
I made a mistake…and wrote this poem.

—written by workshop students

❧ I Hear America Singing ❧

I hear America singing, the varied carols I hear,

Those of mechanics, each one singing his as it should be blithe and
strong,

The carpenter singing his as he measures his plank or beam,

The mason singing his as he makes ready for work, or leaves off work,

The boatman singing what belongs to him in his boat, the deckhand
singing on the steamboat deck,

The shoemaker singing as he sits on his bench, the hatter singing as
he stands,

The wood-cutter's song, the ploughboy's on his way in the morning,
or at noon intermission or at sundown,

The delicious singing of the mother, or of the young wife at work, or
of the girl sewing or washing,

Each singing what belongs to him or her and to none else,

The day what belongs to the day—at night the party of young
fellows, robust, friendly,

Singing with open mouths their strong melodious songs.

—Walt Whitman

FAVORITE POETRY LESSONS
Scholastic Professional Books, 1998

❧ I Hear America Singing ❧

READ THE POEM

I've always admired Walt Whitman's bold sprawling lines, and when I came across *The List Poem* by Larry Fagin, which plays off of "I Hear America Singing," I knew I'd found a wonderful way to entice young writers to appreciate Whitman too. After my students have read Whitman's poem—it works beautifully as a Read Around—I give them a short-lined rhyming version from Fagin's book, which begins:

> I hear America singing
> I hear the bells ringing
> I hear the glasses clinking
> I hear the teachers drinking
> I hear the drivers driving
> I hear the nurses arriving
> I hear the water dripping
> I hear my pants ripping

DISCUSS THE POEM

I ask students to tell me what they notice about the Whitman poem, guiding them to see that the poet is celebrating the ordinary endeavors of everyday folk. We notice how, with a few words, Whitman gives us a snapshot we can picture of each character, and we enjoy his repetition of the word *singing*. Next, we look at the Fagin poem and chuckle at its lighthearted spin on Whitman's subject. I use Fagin's poem to point out that poets throughout time have been playing off of one another, sometimes penning poems that reverently pay tribute to another's work, sometimes gently poking fun.

❧ IN THE POET'S WORDS... ❧

"Rhyme seems to automatically quicken and lighten a poem, regardless of the subject. Sometimes I can't make rhyme convey my feelings. I wish I could! On the other hand, free verse is infinitely more difficult for me. Without boundaries of a rhyme scheme and fixed meter, I find it harder to say what I want with economy."

—Bobbi Katz

> **CRAFT CLOSE-UP:** *Poetic License* This is a good time to talk about poetic license, a term that essentially means that writers can invent "facts" for their poems, provided that they fit in the poem. For example, if students are writing about things they hear in their houses, they can include "I hear our car parking/I hear the poodle barking" even if they do not actually have a dog. Their poems may, in fact, include things that no one can actually hear. For example, "I hear the snow falling," "I hear the babies dreaming," and "I hear the flowers growing." Young writers should not feel bound by the literal when they're creating poems.

WRITE AN INDIVIDUAL POEM

I invite students to try their own versions of a Whitmanesque poem, and I tell them they needn't use America as their subject. I ask them what other places would make suitable locales for their poems. Students often come up with an impressive list, including school, city, house, neighborhood, and their state. I remind them that whatever subject they choose, they should pay close attention to what they might find in that environment. You can see how the excerpt below, from a poem written by a fourth grader, captures a specific setting:

I HEAR THE POND SINGING

> I hear the pond singing
> I hear the water pinging
> I hear the frogs croaking
> I hear a fisher smoking
> I hear the crickets chirping
> I hear the toads burping
> I hear the muskrat swimming
> I hear two beetles skimming
> I hear the fish dining
> I hear the loons whining
> I hear the duck quacking
> I hear the fox snacking
> I hear the sparrow flying
> I hear its call dying
> —Patrick Hanan

Another young poet, captivated by the *Star Wars* saga, wrote:

I hear the rebel alliance singing
I hear light sabers clinging
I hear blasters beaming
I hear Princess Leia screaming
I hear Luke Skywalker learning
I hear dead pilots burning
I hear Yoda dying
I hear Luke and Leia crying
I hear Chewbacca roaring
I hear Imperial fighters soaring
I hear Jabba the Hut snickering
I hear Luke and Hans bickering
I hear control panels dinging
I hear the rebel alliance singing
—Leonard Lang

POETRY LINKS

Social Studies: Students can write a variation of "I Hear America Singing" when they study their own state, another state, or a foreign country, city, or region.

Science: Have students write fact-laced "I Hear" poems about a particular ecosystem, such as the ocean, mountains, forest, swamp, or a river.

Synonym Poems

Rancid

Sour, musty, putrid, rotten

This old trash won't be forgotten.

Outlaw

Pirate, bandit, thief, or crook

At them the judge should throw the book.

Earth

World, planet, one-mooned globe

To other planets we send probes.

Ghost

Spirit, goblin, bogeyman

They will haunt you if they can.

Fast

Swift, speedy, fleet, or quick

Go too fast and you'll make me sick.

—written by workshop students

FAVORITE POETRY LESSONS
Scholastic Professional Books, 1998

❧ Synonym Poems ❧

READ THE POEMS

Because the synonym poem is made up of one couplet—no more, no less—it's a good form for students to work with as they venture into writing short rhyming poems. As with most of my poetry lessons, I begin by handing out a sheet of poems written by other students (use page 32). After students have had time to read the synonym poems to themselves, I ask for volunteers to read them aloud so that everyone can hear the clear rhythms.

DISCUSS THE POEMS

I make the point that the poems are descriptive and that they're made up of words that mean the same thing. I make sure that everyone knows the term *synonym*. Then I divide the class into small groups and give each group a couple of thesauruses. I assign a couple of words to each group and ask them to find some synonyms.

I want the kids to know that the thesaurus is a valuable tool for a writer. But, like any tool, it can be abused. Students might be tempted to use it as a source of "big" words that are not natural to them but are simply words that they feel will "impress" a reader. So for writing their synonym poems, I encourage them to use thesaurus words they know but just hadn't thought of on the spot.

POETRY LINKS

Science: Since the synonym poem is descriptive, it's a good one to use in science, a discipline that requires keen powers of observation and a careful recording of details. Students can write synonym poems about animals, climate, space, or oceans.

Language Arts: Invite students to write collections of synonym poems that describe various emotions—sad, happy, lonely, jealous, in love, angry, confused, joyous, and so on. Find a way to have kids link these "feelings poems" to a character in a novel you're reading.

WRITE A POEM

Now we're ready to write a class poem or two on the board or on chart paper. I don't rush through this drafting, because I want the young writers to experience all the thought processes—about word choice, rhythm, rhyme—that go into writing a poem. Students question, discuss, or argue about the class poems. These conversations are very important, as they give students the opportunity to thrash around with word choices and really understand their effect on each line of a poem. For example, if students are having trouble recognizing rhythm in the class poem they're drafting, I'll point to a line from a synonym poem on the sheet and change a word so that the rhythm gets thrown off course. For example, if you change "Spirit, goblin, bogeyman" to "Phantasm, goblin, bogeyman," the opening line of that poem doesn't flow as smoothly as the original.

Before students begin writing, I review the ingredients of a synonym poem:

➔ A synonym poem is descriptive.

➔ It is always made up of one couplet.

➔ The first line contains three or four synonyms (or descriptive words) for the subject.

➔ The second line either tells how you feel about the subject (for example, "This old trash won't be forgotten") or describes the subject a little more ("They will haunt you if they can").

➔ Each line generally has seven or eight syllables arranged in a way that gives each poem a distinctive rhythm.

CRAFT CLOSE-UP: Word Choice Working with synonyms provides an opportunity to talk about word choice. Ask kids such questions as: Why might it be better to use one word instead of another? Do different words create different moods? Although all the synonyms mean essentially the same thing, why do we react differently when we hear (or use) some of the synonyms? For example, *skinny* and *slender* are synonyms for *thin*. How do we react to those words? Does one have a less appealing connotation than the other? This contrast between connotations of the same word could, incidentally, make for an interesting poem. For example, the students could write a synonym poem using only unpleasant synonyms of a word. For example, the first line of "Thin" might be: "Slight, bony, twiggy, gaunt." And then they could try one with a sunnier spin: "Slender, lithe, willowy."

34

❧ Opposites ❧

What is the opposite of new?
It might be stale gum that's hard to chew,
Or it could be wrinkled and gray;
Most old people are that way.

The opposite of flower
Can easily be told within the hour.
It isn't leaves, a stem, or petals,
But big fat blobs of ugly metal.

What is the opposite of good?
Why, someone mean and nasty: a hood.

What is the opposite of kind?
A goat that butts you from behind.

The opposite of a chair
Is sitting down with nothing there.

What is the opposite of having many?
It is quite obvious: not having any!

—written by workshop students

❧ Opposites ❧

WRITING OPPOSITES

I discovered opposite poems many years ago when I was browsing in a library and found *Opposites,* a book of poems by Richard Wilbur, renowned poet and translator. It was one of those serendipitous things that happens to us now and again. I had used Wilbur's poems in a number of my anthologies and respected his work. A quick thumb-through revealed short poems and lighthearted drawings by the poet. If I had any doubt about using the form of the opposite with my kids—I didn't even know it *was* a form—they vanished when I read:

> What is the opposite of two?
> A lonely me, a lonely you.

After I tried my hand writing opposites and came up with a few suitable poems, one of my favorite poetry activities was born. I tell this story as a reminder that we must be willing to experiment with our poetry lessons. I am constantly encouraging my kids to take a chance by trying something new, and I need to model that attitude in my teaching. With a good knowledge of our students and a willingness to improvise on our own, an exciting new lesson can be created. After I tinkered with my examples and worked on my delivery, my students were writing some wonderful opposites.

READ THE POEM

For a couple of reasons, I usually have my students write opposites after they've done the synonym poems. First of all, it builds on some of the basic concepts they discussed and used while they were writing synonym poems—things like rhythm, rhyme, and couplets. Second, although the opposite is also a short rhyming poem, it requires a higher level of thinking than a synonym poem. While the synonym and the opposite basically describe a subject, their approaches are different. The synonym poem describes what something is or does; the opposite describes what the subject is not! In a sense, the opposite poem is, well, the opposite of a synonym poem.

DISCUSS THE POEM

After students have had time to read over the model poem, "Opposites," we discuss each example and I guide them to notice the following things about an opposite poem:

> → It *is* about opposites.
>
> → It's made of couplets, so it can be two, four, six, eight, or more lines long. (Four lines is a good length because many students find it difficult to sustain the poem beyond that.)

36

→ The first line is frequently, though not always, a question: What is the opposite of _____?

→ If the poem opens with a question, the rest of the poem answers that question.

→ Like all good poems, a good opposite illustrates with specific details.

BRAINSTORM IDEAS

Because opposites require young writers to work at a higher level of thinking, it is especially important to take them slowly through the class poem. Selecting a topic for this type of poem is crucial, because not everything has an opposite. I suggest that students begin by writing an opposite about an adjective. If they choose adjectives like *big, small, tall,* they can easily find opposites such as *little, huge,* and *short.*

CRAFT CLOSE-UP: *Show, Don't Tell* Opposite poems provide a natural opportunity for discussing concrete details that *show* rather than *tell.* You might, for example, have your class make a list of specific things that are the opposite of tall (ants, worms, commas, buttercups) as part of the class poem. Point out that these things *show* the concept of small without telling it and are more fun to read.

WRITE THE POEM

Although it's perfectly all right for my students to write some two-line opposites, I insist that they also write at least one longer poem. They are comfortable writing two-line poems, but I want them to reach beyond what is comfortable.

Some two-line opposites, however, are simply not complete. They need more specifics, more details. Consider this opposite:

> What is the opposite of tall?
> Of course, it's something small.

I would encourage the writer of this opposite to create another couple of lines with details that complete the poem. Perhaps a couplet like this:

> Like mites and gnats and pesky ants
> And other bugs crawling in your pants.

Other opposites, while they are four lines long, may not have the details that we expect in a good poem. For example:

> What is the opposite of taking a nap?
> The answer's really quite a snap.
> Because a nap is what I hate
> The opposite would be great.

While this student seems to have understood the basics of writing an opposite, her poem does not give us a clear picture of something that is opposite of a nap. This writer needs to brainstorm a list of things that she considers "great." From a list filled with details, she might rewrite her opposite something like this:

> What is the opposite of taking a nap?
> The answer's really quite a snap.
> Riding your bike, dancing all night,
> Or smacking a baseball outta sight!

POETRY LINKS

Math: You might ask your students to write an opposite poem about a math concept such as infinity, addition, and geometric figures like a square.

Language Arts: Types of behavior—rude, snotty, kind, fair—often make good topics for opposites.

Social Studies: Deepen kids' understanding of social studies concepts by having them write opposite poems. For example, you might ask them to explore: What is the opposite of war? What is the opposite of bigotry? Of freedom?

❧ Clerihews ❧

Edgar Allan Poe

Was passionately fond of roe

He always liked to chew some

When writing anything gruesome.

Lewis Carroll

Bought sumptuous apparel

And built an enormous palace

Out of the profits of Alice.

The Abbe Liszt

Hit the piano with his fist.

That was the way

He used to play.

Mr. H. G. Wells

Was composed of cells.

He thought the human race

Was a perfect disgrace.

—E. Clerihew Bentley

❧ Clerihews ❧

WRITING CLERIHEWS

The clerihew was invented by E. C. Bentley, a British writer known primarily for his classic mystery novel *Trent's Last Case.* During World War II, Bentley wrote a column for a London newspaper, in which he often included the short humorous poems that he'd invented as a schoolboy.

Just as the opposite is built upon the same concepts utilized in the synonym poem, the clerihew builds on some of those same concepts: couplets, rhythm, humor, and details. But with a twist: Clerihew are about celebrities, as the selections by Bentley show.

READ THE POEM

Bentley's clerihew are somewhat dated and "very British," so I also give my students some clerihew written by their peers from other classes. Copy the following poems on the board or on chart paper:

> Basketball ace, Dr. J
> Is seven feet tall so they say.
> His only hang-up is buying shoes.
> That's why they had to invent canoes.

> That famous lady, Mona Lisa
> Whose smile is a real teaser
> Will never tell this world we're in
> What's behind that fabled grin.

> Kareem Abdul-Jabbar
> Thinks he's best by far.
> But Dr. J puts him to shame
> With moves throughout the game.

> B-ball star, Dr. J
> Is most perfect in every way.
> He, by far, blows Bird away
> Then the crowd screams, "Dr. J!"

FAVORITE POETRY LESSONS
Scholastic Professional Books, 1998

DISCUSS THE POEM

Using Bentley's and the students' poems as our models, we discuss the ingredients of a good clerihew, coming up with a list like this:

→ It is always four lines long, written in two couplets.

→ It is about a celebrity.

→ It pokes gentle fun at that person, much like a political cartoon.

→ The subject's name must be at the end of the first line, so the second line must rhyme with it.

WRITE THE POEM

Just as an opposite poem requires students to think carefully about a subject, so, too, the clerihew requires similar examination. I define "celebrity" loosely, allowing students to write about local celebrities or family members if they wish. To jump-start the writing process, have the class brainstorm celebrity categories—for example, movies and television, sports, music, politics, literature, science—and write the list on the board for ready reference.

As you've probably noticed, I allow my students to modify their clerihews, much the way Bentley modified his own, by beginning with a few words that *identify* the subject. So, a first line might be something like *Basketball ace, Michael Jordan* or *Novel writer, Gary Paulsen.* But I do not permit them to write *There was a basketball star named Shaq* or the like, just a word or two to put the celebrity into some sort of context.

A word of caution: I urge you to remind your students that the purpose of the clerihew is to poke *gentle* fun at a celebrity, not to be nasty. I tell my young writers that we see far too much hurtful behavior in the world; we need not add to it with our poems.

POETRY LINKS

Across the Curriculum: Since the clerihew describes a person, any discipline that involves people can lend itself to writing clerihews. For example, your kids can write clerihews about historical figures, scientists and inventors, and characters in novels and plays. They can write about authors, artists, composers, and musicians. Students may enjoy drawing or painting portraits of their subjects to accompany their poems.

Useless Things

A spout without a hole
A Swiss without a roll
Ladders without rungs
Taste without tongues,

A shepherd without sheep
A horn without a beep
Hockey without sticks
Candles without wicks,

A pier without the sea
A buzz without a bee
A lid without a box
Keys without locks,

A harp without a string
A pong without a ping
A broom without its bristles
Refs without whistles,

A glacier without ice
Ludo without dice
A chair without a seat
Steps without feet,

A hat without a head
A toaster without bread
A riddle without a clue
Me without you.

—Richard Edwards

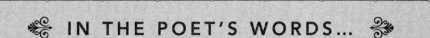

❧ Useless Things ❧

WRITING LONG RHYMING POEMS

When I looked for a long rhyming poem to use as a model for students, I wanted an example laced with humor. I also wanted a poem that followed a pattern and had a unifying theme. "Useless Things," by British poet Richard Edwards, fit the bill.

READ THE POEM

I read it aloud to students and am always gratified by how enthusiastic they are about the form. It's easy for every kid—even the poetically shy ones—to grasp and take for a spin on his own.

DISCUSS THE POEM

I remind students that the poem "Useless Things" is a model that need not be followed as carefully as some of the short rhyming poetic forms we had done. I invite them to write a poem that captures the *spirit* of Edwards' poem.

WRITE THE POEM

After much brainstorming, discussing, writing and rewriting, one group of students presented some humorous variations of "Useless Things," like the one shown on the next page.

> **POETRY LINKS**
>
> **Art:** The nonsensical nature of Useless Things poems lends itself to visual art. Have students look through the "useless" poems to find a line that they could represent with visual art.
>
> **Social Studies:** Students might research some far-fetched or unsuccessful inventions and then write poems.

❧ Can You Imagine? ❧

Rafts that don't float
Castles without moats

A ladder without a rung
Michael Jordan without a tongue

Soda without bubbles
Bart Simpson without troubles

Elephants without trunks
Summer camp without bunks

Birds without feathers
Days without weather

A clock without time
A poem that doesn't rhyme.

—Libby Shapira

FAVORITE POETRY LESSONS
Scholastic Professional Books, 1998

❧ I Like That Stuff ❧

Children play on it
Adults lay on it
Sand
I like that stuff.
—Alexis Heimann

Cats curl in it
Plants unfurl in it
Sun
I like that stuff.
—Christina Perron

Cakes are smothered with it
Twix are covered with it
Chocolate
I like that stuff
—Justin Black

Frowns are fixed by it
Friends are mixed by it
Smiles
I like that stuff
—Sophie Northway

❧ I Like That Stuff ❧

WRITING COLLABORATIVE POEMS

"I Like That Stuff" is modeled after a poem called "Stufferation" by Adrian Mitchell, a British poet and anthologist. I discovered the poem in his collection *Strawberry Drums* and was captivated by its form. I immediately began wondering whether it would work as a model for kids and speculated that it would be a great example for writing collaborative poems and for using refrains. Indeed, it's been a favorite of students.

READ THE POEM

Read aloud the poem to students, or have them take turns reading each stanza. You might also wish to have pairs of students read it aloud, one reading the stanzas, the other the refrain.

DISCUSS THE POEM

Ask your students: What holds this poem together? Guide them to see that the stanzas, which describe different things, are stitched together by the refrain "I like that stuff." Explain that a refrain is a word or phrase that repeats throughout the poem. Now invite them to look more closely at the opening couplet of each stanza. What do they notice? Help students to recognize that the rhyme is not just a simple, one-syllable rhyme, known as a *masculine rhyme*. Here, the rhyme is *feminine*, which means that many syllables within the couplet rhyme. For example, notice how several syllables are part of these rhymes: *play on it/lay on it*; *curl in it/unfurl in it*; *smothered with it/covered with it*.

Through your discussion, you and your students can develop a list that describes the poem's pattern:

> ✦ Each stanza is four lines.

> ✦ Each stanza begins with a couplet.

> ✦ The opening couplets have similar syntax.

> ✦ The third line is the subject of the stanza.

> ✦ The last line in each stanza functions as a refrain.

WRITING THE POEM

The form of Adrian Mitchell's poem makes an excellent model for a collaborative piece, for which individuals, pairs, or small groups of students can contribute a stanza. You might even offer your kids the chance to turn the poem on its head by using the refrain "I hate that stuff." When I did that with a group of seventh graders, one student wrote this stanza:

46

Girls shape their nails with it
You can carve details with it
Files
I hate that stuff.
                    —Steven Burnell

Perhaps you and your students could think up other refrains, such as *I miss that stuff* or *I need that stuff*.

POETRY LINKS

Science: Have students use this type of poem to convey their understanding of various science topics and concepts. For example: *Birds fly south for it/salmon swim the river mouth for it/Migration/I like that stuff.*

Language Arts: Students could show what they know about new vocabulary words by weaving them into poems. Groups of students could collaborate on a longer poem that defines several vocabulary words from a novel or textbook.

❧ Ten Little Aliens ❧

Ten little aliens landed feeling fine
One bought a hot tub and then there were nine.

Nine little aliens stayed up very late
One overslept and then there were eight.

Eight little aliens took the name of Kevin
One died laughing and then there were seven.

Seven little aliens studied magic tricks
One disappeared and then there were six.

Six little aliens learned how to drive
One missed the exit and then there were five.

Five little aliens polished the floor
One slipped and fell and then there were four.

Four little aliens climbed a tall tree
One lost his grip and then there were three.

Three little aliens visited the zoo
One liked the ape and then there were two.

Two little aliens baked in the sun
One got well-done and then there was one.

One little alien went looking for fun
He never came back and now there are none.

—Paul B. Janeczko

❧ Ten Little Aliens ❧

READ THE POEM

Of all the poems that I've written and read to school children, the one that gets the most enthusiastic response is "Ten Little Aliens." I hope that when you read the poem you'll see why kids love hearing it and why they are enthusiastic about writing their own versions. (And, by the way, when a class responds heartily to a poem when it is read aloud, nine times out of ten you'll see wonderful writing results too.)

DISCUSS THE POEM

The pattern in "Ten Little Aliens" is more complex than the other rhyming poems I've presented thus far, but after students have had practice writing other patterned verse, they are ready for the challenge.

So, together, we examine "Ten Little Aliens" and develop the following list of characteristics::

→ The poem is made up of couplets:

→ The first line of each couplet begins with a number; the second line ends with that number minus one.

→ The second line begins with *One*.

→ In the first line, a group of some sort does something.

→ In the second line, something happens to one member of the group, and as a result, there is one fewer. These two parts of the line are joined by the conjunction *and*.

WRITE THE POEM

Although many students—especially boys—regard writing about aliens as the crème de la crème writing assignment, I assure the class that their poems do not have to be about aliens. I wrote about aliens because…well, I'm not quite sure why I wrote about them, except that perhaps I found funny the possibility of what visitors from outer space might do in my poem.

I also encourage kids to work with any number they like. They can write "Six Bratty Brothers" or "Eight Mean Sisters" if they wish. And they have! In fact, I've had students who used "Ten Little Aliens" as a model for poems about: ten little hamsters, kittens, pigs, hairy robbers, rodents, lizards, frogs, skiers, crazy drivers, soccer players.

On the next page, you'll find a delightful example written by two fourth grade boys.

❧ Ten Little Hamsters ❧

Ten little hamsters climbed up a pine
One saw the cat and then there were nine.

Nine little hamsters went on a date
One got married and then there were eight.

Eight little hamsters dashed to a 7-11
One ate a slurpie and then there were seven.

Seven little hamsters got their kicks
One misunderstood and then there were six.

Six little hamsters played near a hive
One got stung and then there were five.

Five little hamsters were all in a bore
One played with the vacuum and then there were four.

Four little hamsters played around a tree
One didn't say, "Timber!," and then there were three.

Three little hamsters went to the zoo
One took a whiff and then there were two.

Two little hamsters played in the sun
One got baked and then there was one.

One little hamster held up a ton
He lost his grip and now there are none.

—Eric Newton

EXTEND THE LESSON

A young writer once asked if he could start his poem with one figure and have another one join the group in each couplet. I was skeptical but told the student that he could certainly try. Well, as is so often the case with young writers, this boy followed his imagination and wrote a fun poem, which began:

> One little alien went to the zoo
> He found his brother and then there were two.
>
> Two little aliens cut down a tree
> They called for help and then there were three.

This reminded me to stay wide open to students' creative twists. We never know how or whether an idea will work until we put the words down, so let's encourage kids to fool around on paper. When we make a mistake or don't care for what we wrote, we can erase and start again. Kids need to be reminded of that. No writers I know write a perfect poem or a perfect novel without making changes—in most cases, lots of changes. Thinking and noodling is a key part of the process, much the way a jazz musician noodles on the piano, or a watercolor painter noodles with sketch pad and pencil.

❧ IN THE POET'S WORDS... ❧

"I often think that I started writing poetry at such an early age because of my stuttering, but I probably would have come to it eventually, speech defect or not, because I became addicted to the freedom of the page, to saying whatever I wanted without having to think about what other people thought. Eventually, I did have to be concerned with that, but early on, it was just me and the paper, that paper that didn't make fun of what I said or how I felt."

—Jim Daniels

If I Could Grant a Wish for You

If I could grant a wish for you,
I would get a thrill or two.

May all your lucky numbers win the lottery
May you discover beautiful, ancient pottery.

May you be able to act and sing
May life bring you every good thing.

May you be able to pig out and not get fat
May you get a hit every time at bat.

May you never get sick or have the flu
May you only have good dreams that come true.

May you be able to do anything you desire
May you never have car trouble or a flat tire.

May you eat chocolate and candy too
May each dish of ice cream be just for you.

May your tests and report cards show great grades
May your room be cleaned by fast-working maids.

May you always have money and never be poor
May you always have peace and never know war.

Oh, if I could grant a wish for you,
I would get a thrill or two.

—Elizabeth Harris

FAVORITE POETRY LESSONS
Scholastic Professional Books, 1998

❧ If I Could Grant a Wish for You ❧

WRITING WISH POEMS

Most of the poems I share with young writers are culled from books and literary journals. However, this poem was written by a sixth-grade girl in a poetry workshop I conducted some years ago. I had distributed copies of my poem, "If I Could Put a Curse on You," a playful, exaggerated poem that is another favorite among middle school kids. A girl asked if she could turn it around and write a poem about granting wishes for people. I smiled and told her that I liked the idea and that she should give it a try. She did. When I read Elizabeth's poem, it was one of those delicious moments that lets me know I'm in the right business. "If I Could Grant a Wish for You" is a poem that I have been using in writing workshops with young poets ever since.

DISCUSS THE POEM

"If I Could Grant a Wish for You" utilizes some of the concepts and terms that we've been talking about, such as couplet and rhyme. Because Elizabeth's poem is not rhythmically perfect, it offers a good opportunity to discuss rhythm with your students. Rhythm is sound—feeling the beat of the words. I think the best way of addressing rhythm is by reading the poem aloud. After students have heard the poem a few times, you might ask them to discuss which words they might change to improve some of the couplets. Perhaps give small groups of writers a few couplets to consider. After they've made some changes to the poem, ask them to read it aloud, giving the class a chance to hear if the rhythm of the poem has been improved.

WRITE THE POEM

When I share Elizabeth's poem with students, I invite them to keep her opening and closing couplets but to recreate all the couplets in between. During the drafting process, I encourage students to read their couplets aloud to a writing partner, to check on the rhythm of the poem. And as I walk around the room checking the students' work, I'm always on the lookout for good rhythmic couplets that I can read aloud to the class.

POETRY LINKS

Writing: "If I Could Grant a Wish for You" makes a perfect gift poem for Mother's Day, Father's Day, Valentine's Day, or a birthday. Or, simply as a gift for someone special. The poem could be part of a decorative card or written on a small poster and delivered in a jazzy, colorful envelope.

Literature: Students who are particularly taken by a character in a story or novel, like Matthais or Cluny from the Redwall books, or Anastasia, could write a wish poem for that character. An array of such poems, with or without illustrations, would make a dazzling bulletin board display.

Social Studies: Students could write a wish poem to a historical figure they admire.

REMEMBER, POETRY IS PLAY

I hope that you find some rhyming poems that will work with the young writers in your class. Although many of these poems follow a specific pattern or form, I offer them as guides, not as shackles. No one knows your students as well as you do, so feel free to pick and choose how these poems will work with your kids. Feel free, as well, to modify them. The important thing is to let the kids see that poetry writing is play. Serious play at times, but play nonetheless. We need to give kids the chance feel the joy and power that comes from working with their language.

FAVORITE POETRY LESSONS
Scholastic Professional Books, 1998

Worth Reading

Myra Cohn Livingston offers good advice and suggestions about rhyme and rhythm in her book *Poem-Making: Ways to Begin Writing Poetry* (HarperCollins, 1991).

One of the finest practitioners of riotous rhyming poetry for young readers is X. J. Kennedy. In addition to his books of poems, he also put together, with his wife Dorothy M. Kennedy, *Knock at a Star: A Child's Introduction to Poetry* (Little, Brown, 1982).

Two books published by Teachers & Writers Collaborative that deserve a spot on your shelf are *The List Poem* by Larry Fagin and *The Teachers & Writers Collaborative Handbook of Poetic Forms*.

There are a number of fine magazines that publish children's poetry. Ones worth exploring are: *Highlights for Children, Spider, Cricket, Lady Bug, New Moon,* and *Merlyn's Pen.*

If you're looking for good rhyming poetry for young readers, feast your eyes and ears on some of these titles:

Bing Bang Boing by Douglas Florian (Harcourt, 1994).

Making Friends With Frankenstein by Colin McNaughton (Candlewick, 1994).

The Other Side of the Door by Jeff Moss (Bantam, 1991).

Please Don't Squeeze Your Boa, Noah! by Marilyn Singer (Holt, 1995).

Poems of A. Nonny Mouse by Jack Prelutsky (Knopf, 1989).

Ridicholas Nicholas by J. Patrick Lewis (Dial, 1995).

Uncle Switch: Loony Limericks by X. J. Kennedy (McElderry, 1997).

You Know Who by John Ciardi (Boyds Mills, 1991).

Writing Free Verse

For the most part, the poems in this section do not rhyme. Some of your writers might miss the safety net of rhythm and rhyme, but, as I constantly remind students, they will not grow as poets unless they take risks. I've found that even the most rhyme-addicted students develop a taste for free verse within a few lessons.

SOUND IN A FREE VERSE POEM

A free verse poem is free of any set rhyme and rhythm, which is not to say that they have no rhythm or rhyme. They do, but it differs from that of a rhymed poem. The rhythm might, for example, speed up or slow down in spots because of the length of the lines or the words used. Sections of smoothly flowing lines might be followed by more staccato sections. And while there will not be end rhyme in a free verse poem, the good poet will work with the sounds of words to create music in a poem. Here are some techniques to share with your students:

assonance: using identical vowel sounds, like the o sound in words like *roses* and *golden* or the *e* sound in *sleep* and *green*.

consonance: using the same final consonant sound, like *up* and *drip* or *pain* and *bone*.

alliteration: using the same initial consonant sound, like *picture perfect play* or *daring deed*.

onomatopoeia: using words that are like sound effects, such as *boom, whoosh,* and *pop*.

Of course, there are other techniques, but these are probably the ones you will use most often. I encourage you to direct your efforts toward guiding kids to write vibrant poetry rather than to nail down poetic techniques and terms.

WORTH READING

If you're looking for more information about the sound of poetry, you can consult any of these:

The Art and Craft of Poetry by Michael J. Bugeja (Writer's Digest Books, 1507 Dana Avenue, Cincinnati, OH 45207, 1994).

In the Palm of Your Hand: The Poet's Portable Workshop by Steve Kowitt (Tilbury House Publishers, 132 Water Street, Gardiner, ME 04345, 1995).

The Poet's Handbook by Judson Jerome (Writer's Digest Books, 1986).

Writing Poems by Robert Wallace, Michelle Boisseau (Addison-Wesley Pub. Co., 1996).

🕮 IN THE POET'S WORDS... 🕮

"Some people think poetry is artificial, a needless attempt to impose a form on language. Oh No! What if there is a most natural, most effective way to say anything you want to say? What if you let yourself seek that most natural way, most effective way? The result will be your best language, no matter how you find it, no matter whether it rhymes or doesn't, and no matter—to tell the truth—whether it is 'correct' or not."

—W. S. Merwin

UNDERSTANDING LINE BREAK

Another aspect of free verse that young writers need to learn about is line break. At first, much of students' free verse will look like prose. They will ask, "How do we know where to end the line?" Unlike rhyming poetry, there really is no rule for line break. There is only this bit of advice: Words that belong together, that somehow make sense together, should be placed together on a line. That might mean six words or a dozen words or only one word. That might mean a complete sentence or a phrase.

While poets have many reasons for breaking lines the way they do, there are a few reasons that seem most prominent:

> ➢ It is logical to break after a sentence or phrase.

> ➢ You might want to emphasize a word or phrase by putting it at the end of a line.

> ➢ Line breaks can be used in place of punctuation.

> ➢ A line break in an unexpected place can help create surprise or humor or irony in a poem.

> ➢ Line breaks may be part of the organic shape of a poem.

Knowing where to break lines takes practice. Read and write free verse with your students, and continually ask them why they think the poet has placed words where he or she has.

LINE-BREAK PRACTICE

To introduce line break, I often take a free verse poem—either mine or one by a poet students are familiar with—and rewrite it to look like prose. I change none of the words or punctuation. I merely "un-arrange" the poem to look like a paragraph. Here's what I do with "The Big Field" by Donald Graves (see page 60).

Mr. Gammons mows the big field with his tractor, then rakes and bundles hay for the barn. George and I grab our bats, gloves, and balls and race across the field like major leaguers in spring training. We hit long flies to each other all afternoon, never lose a ball in the stubble, and don't stop until Mother calls us for supper.

I make an overhead transparency of the unarranged poem and project it onto the screen. I read it aloud a couple of time, so that kids can begin to see and hear how some words go together. Then, marker in hand, I ask the kids to tell me where they think a line break should go. I stand and wait until a timid voice rises from the corner, suggesting I put a line break wherever there is punctuation. An astute observation. I mark those line breaks with a slash, and wait as others begin to feel the sense of the poem and suggest other line breaks.

After I've added as many line breaks as they're willing to suggest, I ask students to take a good look at their work one last time. Then I project the poem onto the screen so that students can see the way the poet broke the lines.

The Big Field

Mr. Gammons mows the big field

with his tractor,

then rakes and bundles

hay for the barn.

George and I

grab our bats,

gloves, and balls

and race across the field

like major leaguers

in spring training.

We hit long flies

to each other

all afternoon,

never lose a ball

in the stubble,

and don't stop

until Mother calls

us for supper.

—Donald Graves

FAVORITE POETRY LESSONS
Scholastic Professional Books, 1998

MORE LINE-BREAK POINTERS

Most of the time, students can do a good job suggesting line breaks, especially if the poems you use as examples lend themselves to somewhat logical line breaks. Other poems that have worked well for me are:

→ "Sam, the Shoe Shop Man" by Cynthia Rylant (*Waiting to Waltz*)

→ "Grandpa's Shoes" by Deborah Chandra (*Rich Lizard and Other Poems*)

→ "For You" by Karla Kuskin (*Near the Window Tree*)

Of course, we all know that many students are frequently more skilled at looking critically at someone else's work than they are at carefully examining their own. And, since writing free verse is a new skill for many of your students, you will need to remind them to look for places to put line breaks in their own poems. I tell my students that there is no law telling them that the first draft of a free verse poem needs to look like a poem. If they wish to write their drafts simply as a block of text, that's okay. When they've completed their first drafts, they can simply draw slash marks where they think the line breaks should go. The next step is to copy that draft onto a fresh sheet of paper, breaking the lines where they've indicated.

Introducing Free Verse Writing

Free verse does not have the structure that rhymed poetry has, so I take a somewhat different approach when I present it to my students. I hand out a sheet of model poems. We read the poems aloud and discuss noteworthy aspects. However, when my students write a free verse poem, we skip collaborating on a class poem, in part because this kind of poetry doesn't have explicit structure to master in a warm-up, and in part because my students, having written a number of rhyming poems, are more able to jump right into their own verse.

The activities in this part of the book do not include checklists like the activities for rhymes. Most of those checklists concerned a structure that is absent in most free verse poems. However, there are some questions you can ask of students when they write free verse poems:

→ Have they chosen a topic that means something to them?

→ Have they shared the draft with someone who can offer constructive suggestions to improve the poem?

→ Have they used details that create an image that appeals to the senses of a reader?

→ Have they read the poem aloud to a writing partner as they both listen to the sound of the words?

→ Have they truly revised their poem—looked at it again—until they are satisfied with it?

🙠 IN THE POET'S WORDS... 🙢

"The purpose of a poem [is] to give shape in a concise and memorable way to what our lives feel like. In this way, poems help us to notice the world more and better, and they enable us to share with others, who may be still looking for the right words, the words we have found, through art, to express many of the deepest and subtlest aspects of our experience."

—Jonathan Holden

❧ Acrostic Poems ❧

Daniel

Does not
Allow any
Nagging or
Insults to get to him.
Everyone
Likes his big eyes.

Brother

Bossy
Rowdy
Ordering me
To do
His bidding.
Eager to
Run my life.

Sister

Sometimes
Ignores me
So much
That I
Eventually
Roar.
   —written by workshop students

❧ Acrostic Poems ❧

WORD CHOICE AND PLACEMENT

There are a couple of reasons that I like to introduce free verse with an acrostic poem. It's a format that any student can successfully write, and it helps kids begin to realize the importance of word choice and word placement in a free verse poem. True, these aspects of an acrostic poem are contrived—the students need to find words that start with certain letters—but the format nonetheless shows young writers that they cannot use any word in any place they choose.

READ THE POEMS

After we read the poems, I ask students to think about how they're alike and how they're different. I tell them that although these poems are all written about family members, an acrostic can be about any subject.

DISCUSS THE POEMS

As the samples show, there are basically two ways to write an acrostic poem. One way is to write something of a list poem, like "Brother," which lists four qualities of the subject of the poem. A second approach is to write a single sentence that wraps its way through the poem, like "Sister." A variation of these types is an acrostic that combines a list and a sentence.

WRITE THE POEM

To get students started, I often invite them to write an acrostic about themselves. I suggest that they begin by writing their name at the top of the page, then down the left-hand margin, one letter per line. I discourage them from looking at the letters and trying to think of something about themselves that will fit with each letter. It's generally not productive for a student to look at her name and think, "Oh, I'll never think of anything about myself that begins with Y!" or "What can I possibly say about me that begins with D?" That will produce more staring than writing. Rather, I tell them to think about themselves and brainstorm a list

PAUL

THINGS I LIKE

- JAZZ
- READING
- BASEBALL
- ROCK + ROLL - OLD STUFF
- PIZZA
- MEXICAN FOOD
- GOING TO THE MOVIES
- LISTENING TO EMMA READ
- SUMMER

of the things that make them unique. Then they can look for ways to work those ideas into the poem. To illustrate that point, I begin to draft a poem about myself on the board.

I draw circles around jazz, rock & roll, and Mexican food. I tell the kids, "These are three things about me that I want to include in my acrostic. But none of them starts with a letter in my name. What should I do? Give up on them? Instead, I'll work them in like this:

PAUL

Prefers jazz
And good old rock & roll.
Usually on the
Lookout for Mexican food.

Before students begin drafting their acrostic poems, we talk about the kinds of things they might want to include. We write a list on the board: likes, dislikes, hobbies, family, school, sports, personality traits. I tell kids that they can take one passion in their lives—like sports, music, or reading—and make that the basis of their poem (like a seventh-grade girl in one of my workshops whose acrostic poem about herself was filled with all the reasons she hated school!).

Most students will get the hang of writing an acrostic poem pretty quickly. I ask those kids who finish their poems to write another one, perhaps about another aspect of their lives. Or they might want to write about a friend or someone in their family. I also suggest that they write acrostic poems about themselves choosing different names or different personalities.

POETRY LINKS

The acrostic poem is versatile, which gives you the opportunity to work it into other curricular areas. Students can, for example, write a poem about a character in social studies, literature, or science.

What to Do in Rudd, Iowa

Go to Hoover's Hatchery and watch eggs hatch.

Count the drops of water leaking from the water tower within one
  hour and calculate

how much water will be lost in one year.

Try to drive on every street in town in under three minutes.

See how fast you can go over the railroad tracks without hitting
  your head on the roof of the car.

Try to guess the weight of the next load of corn or beans brought
  into the elevator.

Watch the firemen polish the fire trucks.

Try to find ten people who pronounce Rudd incorrectly.

On garbage days you see how many people use brown bags and
  how many use black bags.

Go to the creek and count fish.

Go to the store and watch the trucks unload.

—John Grosshoeme and K. McCullough

What to Do in Rudd, Iowa

WRITING LIST POEMS

Were I forced to bring but one of my folders of poems to a school visit, I would grab the one stuffed with list poems. They are unusually accessible, allowing all students to succeed, and they have a noble history, dating back to the Bible and including the work of, among others, poets like Walt Whitman and Allen Ginsburg. Most list poems are unrhymed, but, as you've seen with "I Hear America Singing" and "Useless Things," kids can write rhyming list poems as well. They can be long or short, with long, sprawling lines or short lines like a grocery shopping list.

READ THE POEM

I like to start off list-poem writing by giving students a couple of sheets with half a dozen examples. The first poem on the handout is "What to Do in Rudd, Iowa" by John Grosshoeme and K. McCullough, a couple of high school students. Other models that I share illustrate variations of the list poem: "Things That Go Away & Come Back Again" by Anne Waldman and "Things to Do if You Are the Rain" by Bobbi Katz. In addition, I share student poems with such titles as "Things That Drive Me Crazy," "Things My Sister Does That I Hate," "When I'm Alone I . . .," and "Things That Make Me Look."

DISCUSS THE POEM

I have used "What to Do in Rudd, Iowa" in workshops with students in grades 4 through 12 from Maine to Alaska as well as in England and Germany, in rural and urban schools, in large and small schools, and when I ask students, "What's it like living in Rudd, Iowa?," the response is always the same: "Boring!" I act incredulous and say, "How can you possibly say it's boring living in Rudd, Iowa? The poets don't use that word. They don't use dull or uninteresting or unexciting or any other synonyms for boring. How do you get the idea that it is boring living in that town?" The response is usually a variation of "Because of the things they put in the poem!" "Ahhh," I say, suddenly enlightened. "You mean because of the details in the poem?" "Yes!" "You mean, the poets *show* us it is boring in their town instead of merely *telling* us it is boring?"

There is usually a stunned silence as they realize they have recognized something that I have encouraged them to do in their writing from day one.

So, despite some things in this poem that could benefit from more revising, it's a wonderful example of show-don't-tell and a good model for students as they write their own What-to-Do list poem about their home city, town, or neighborhood.

"A History of the Pets" by David Huddle (page 68) is another favorite model.

❧ A History of the Pets ❧

Butch, a black cocker spaniel, collected

stinks, dirt, and open wounds into which our

father poured gentian violet. Did not

come back one morning. A brown and white mutt

—I don't recall its name—shot by our

mother, beheaded, and pronounced rabid

by health folks who provided all five of us

with fourteen Friday nights of shots. There was

Hooker, half-Persian cat who'd claw your back-

side through the open backed kitchen chairs and swing

by his hooks till you pulled him loose. Rabbits.

Small possums loose in the house. Short-Circuit,

affectionate cat that walked crooked, that'd been

BB-shot in the head. Goat. Skunk. Some snakes.

—David Huddle

FAVORITE POETRY LESSONS
Scholastic Professional Books, 1998

❧ A History of the Pets ❧

DISCUSS THE POEM

Kids love this poem. When I ask them what Huddle is describing, they immediately see that he is describing his family's pets. Then I ask, "Do you get a picture of anything else as you read this poem?," guiding them to look beyond the literal. I give them time to reread it. Usually, many students see that Huddle also gives the reader a picture of what the household was like. This is probably not a neat and tidy house, they realize, not with this menagerie of odd pets running around. I remind the young writers that a good poem suggests rather than states.

Since I only had two pets in my life (both dogs), including the current family hound, I wouldn't try to write a history of my pets. Many students might feel the same. But the history poem is a wonderful list poem that has other applications. Kids can write a history poem about houses they've lived in, schools they've attended, friends they've had, things they've done to get in trouble. In other words, a history poem traces some theme through at least part of a writer's life. A seventh-grade girl wrote the delightful history poem on the next page, which I use as an example of how a poem accrues vividness through very specific details—the names of the shoes, their color, and what happened to each pair.

WRITE THE POEM

One way to help students get an idea for a history poem is to ask them to write "I Remember" at the top of a notebook page and then write down any memories that spring to mind. Those two words at the top of the page will likely get them started remembering some of the funny, scary, important things in their lives. Once they've had sufficient time to write a list (a number of five- or ten-minute opportunities over a week or two), ask them to see if they can find any recurring themes—certain things, places, or feelings that they notice again and again. Another strategy is to give them some journal writing or prewriting prompts that will offer them the chance to do some remembering in specific areas. For example, what can they remember about school, travel, pets, accidents, dreams?

❧ A History of the ❧ Faulty Shoes

Tiny white lacy slippers
    that I kicked off when I was a baby
Sweet little pink jellies
    that I wore on the swing set and broke the strap
Soft leather moccasins
    that had beads that fell off
Bright pink sneakers
    that were hard to lace up
Little purple velcro tennis shoes
    that had a hole in the heel
Shiny black party shoes
    that got scratched on the sidewalk
White leather sandals
    that got wet in the sprinkler and shrank
Green all-stars
    that rubbed at the toe
Black Mary-Janes
    that I still wear today
But who knows?

—Amanda Granum

FAVORITE POETRY LESSONS
Scholastic Professional Books, 1998

❦ How to Make a Snow Angel ❦

Go alone or with a best friend.
Find a patch of unbroken snow.

Walk on tiptoes. Step backwards
Into your very last footprints.

Slowly sit back onto the snow,
Absolutely do not use your hands.

By now you should be lying flat
With snow fitting snug around you.

Let your eyes drink some blue sky.
Close them. Breathe normally.

Move your arms back and forth.
Concentrate. Think: snow angel.

In a minute don't be surprised
If you start feeling a little funny.

Both big and small. Warm and cold.
Your breath light as a snowflake.

Sweep your legs back and forth
But keep both eyes tightly closed.

Keep moving the arms until they
Lift, tremble, wobble or float.

Stand without using your hands.
Take time to get your balance.

Take three deep breaths.
Open your eyes.

Stretch. Float. Fly!

—Ralph Fletcher

❧ How to Make a Snow Angel ❧

READ THE POEM

A third variation of the list poem is the how-to poem. I always use Ralph Fletcher's "How to Make a Snow Angel" as a wonderful example of this form.

DISCUSS THE POEM

Fletcher's poem illustrates a how-to poem that follows steps in a process. When I asked students for other possible processes that might make a good subject for a how-to poem, they suggested: How to make a peanut butter sandwich, How to make a hot fudge sundae, How to fall in love, How to get someone to fall in love with you, How to (not) do homework. When looking for a topic for a how-to poem, it's important for students to find a subject that is simple but lets them incorporate their own personalities. For example, making a peanut butter and jelly sandwich is a simple enough process, but how can the writer make that process special? Perhaps with a unique way of spreading the peanut butter or jelly. Or perhaps with a poetic way of describing the process of spreading the peanut butter. The how-to poem, in other words, must be more than simply a recipe or a set of instructions.

WRITE THE POEM

A good list poem is more than a list; it has to carry the specific details that we expect in other kinds of poems. Each word must be chosen, considered, tweaked, or replaced until the poet senses that every line is taut and yet bouncy as a trampoline. Attention must be given to the order of the words and phrases in a list poem. Will you move from small things to more important things? If you're writing about "things I hear in the morning," you might arrange your list poem in chronological order. On the next page, notice how an eighth-grade student organized her poem in a roughly chronological order. Notice, too, how her poem ends in a way that brings it full circle.

POETRY LINKS

Brainstorm with the whole class or small groups to find things and ideas they might include in a list poem about quietness or beauty, things I wish I could do, musicians or historical figures I would like to meet.

Science topics—like climate, electricity, energy—are filled with technical language. Students can write a list poem that features the music of such terms.

FAVORITE POETRY LESSONS
Scholastic Professional Books, 1998

❧ When I am Alone I... ❧

think about my life
it's gone up in smoke
cry
listen to my cat
hear music play
hold my breath
scream
sleep
never dream
sing along
clean
hold my breath
watch the news
have some coffee
fix a meal
do the dishes
sweep the floor
strum my guitar
mess up and start again

—Ollie Dodge

Old Farm in Northern Michigan

Barn, you have leaned too far

trying for those wormy apples.

Now your cows will never come back

and fill their pails with cream.

Now the horse will never come back

with its hot breath and sweaty collar.

Barn, you have leaned too far—

even the cat thinks you are crazy

and stays close to the car.

—Gary Gildner

❧ IN THE POET'S WORDS... ❧

"A poem is one of those places where you can write about things that you know and feel are true without worrying about whether they are 'real' in the ordinary sense. Poems can represent what another poet calls 'heart-truths'—feelings and experiences out of our deepest selves."

—Gregory Orr

❧ Old Farm in Northern Michigan ❧

READ THE POEM

It is important that your students understand that a poem of address is a poem *to* something or somebody, not simply *about* that object or person. Instead of saying something like, "I saw a dilapidated barn," a poet might consider addressing the building itself, as Gary Gildner did in "Old Farm in Northern Michigan."

DISCUSS THE POEM

As far as the subject of a poem of address is concerned, the possibilities are endless. Students can choose the spectacular or the commonplace. They can write a poem to a person they admire but have never met. (We all have fantasized about what we would say to an athlete, writer, or public figure if we only had the chance to meet him or her.) Or the person they admire could be their parent, sibling, or neighbor. They can write a poem of thanks. The poem of address seems to work well if students try to write to a person with whom they have unfinished business. Perhaps the person has died, moved away, or stopped being a friend, and the writer never got the chance to say some things she held in her heart, as this young writer did:

> Grandmother
> O, Yaya, I miss you.
> I know I never enjoyed
> our Sunday lunches with you
> inside the dining room
> not out in the sun.
> You were old
> I was young.
> I never talked to you,
> unless I was forced

but I didn't know
how much I loved you.
Now, you are gone
I miss our lunches,
the dining room empty,
the chairs pushed in tight.
And the maid has left.
So have you
and I wish you'd come back
因 because I miss you.
—Kate Manthos

One of the reasons I like this poem is the detail that the poet used in telling her story. My favorite detail is "the chairs pushed in tight," which emphasizes the emptiness of the room. But she uses other details to contrast her feelings then and now—for example, being inside and wanting to be "out in the sun" and not talking "unless I was forced." From these rich, telling details come the emotions of the young writer. When the poet read this poem to her mother, Yaya's daughter, the woman was totally surprised by what the girl had written because she had never expressed any of those feelings at the time of Yaya's death, some ten months earlier.

❧ IN THE POET'S WORDS... ❧

"When 'inspiration' comes, the best way to be ready is to have spent many hours, years even, working on less-than-inspired poems. Then the lucky moment arrives, and the craft you have practiced so patiently will flow into place supporting and carrying your poem to its finest possible fulfillment."

—Joan LaBombard

WRITE THE POEM

I tell my students that to write a good poem of address, a poet needs to study his subject very carefully before he begins to write. If you want to write a poem to your toddler brother, get down on all fours, and see what life is like on that level. To write a poem to your pet snake, you need to look at that animal and think what it means to you, what you'd like to ask it, what you'd like to say to it. On page 78 is a poem written by a seventh-grade boy to an ordinary, everyday object. Notice how he has observed the object and had some fun with the poem.

76

CRAFT CLOSE-UP: *Write From the Heart*

If we ask our students to write from the heart, we must be prepared for what they give us. They may tell jolly stories, but they may also tell stories that worry us. In some cases, their stories might necessitate that we talk with the student or have a school counselor talk with him or her. Some teachers may not wish to assume such responsibility. However, writing from the heart often gives kids the chance to unburden themselves in a way they never have before.

At nearly every residency I've conducted, a teacher has come up to me after reading student poems or hearing them read in class and said with surprise, "I never expected that from him (or her)." Most often, the teacher is talking about a "troublemaker" or an "unmotivated" student. But I am never surprised when a disenfranchised student writes some wonderfully angry or sensitive poetry. Poetry writing often gives a student a voice that he may feel doesn't work for him in prose. And there is often a certain nonconformist feel to poetry that kids on the fringe—academically or socially—take to with gusto. On some days you can feel their empowerment. So can the people around them.

During a recent residency at a middle school, a woman walked into my room the morning of my third day while I was getting ready for students to arrive. She was a faculty member at the school as well as the mother of a sixth grader.

"I have to tell you something," she said after introducing herself. "Yesterday my son was in your writing workshop. After school he had soccer practice so he came home sweaty and messy. While he was taking his bath, he started reciting the poems he had written in your workshop. My second-grade son was in awe. 'Did you write all those poems?' he asked. My older son proudly said he had. And I just wanted to thank you for putting something into his heart."

As flattered as I was by her words, I had to tell her that I hadn't put anything in her son's heart. It was there all along. All he needed was the opportunity and permission to let it out. Poetry is like that. It can let kids—and adults, if we let it—speak from the heart. And, sad to say, kids, especially junior high and older kids, don't get enough opportunities to do that in school districts that have become obsessed with assessment and test scores.

I'M SORRY, PENCIL

I know it must be hard
for you to be
a pencil.
It must be hard
having your head rubbed
against a sheet of paper
every single day.
It must be hard
for your rear to rub
on the remains
of your head.
It also must be hard
to be sharpened
because it slices off your skin.
For that
I am sorry
but I ask you
how would I write then?
—Michael Dolce

The poem of address offers many opportunities to introduce poetry in other disciplines. Kids could write poems to people in history or literature. On the following page is a poem written by a middle school writer to a famous character in literature.

LITTLE WHITE RABBIT

Why did you confuse Alice so?

She was just fine until you beckoned
for her to come through the mirror.

And why, oh WHY did you you keep
her running after you
as though it was some marathon

If it were my choice,

I'd have thrown you in a fireplace

(Because I know you hate
to be dirty)

Until you turned black with soot…

And I heard Alice needs
a new rabbit's foot!

—Kristin Hardin

LETTER POEM

A first cousin of the poem of address is the letter poem, in which the poem is written as a letter. Lilian Moore wrote her letter poem to a friend.

POETRY LINKS

Language Arts: The poem of address and the letter poem work especially well when written to a person the student might actually like to write a letter to— such as an author or a character they admire in a book or movie, like Lyddie, Rifka, or Anastasia. A word of caution, however. Young writers need to be constantly reminded that, despite the conversational tone of many letter poems, they still require attention to the nuts and bolts of good poetry: word choice, rhythm, images, and so on.

Social Studies: The letter poem is a perfect vehicle for young writers who wish to explore the culture and heritage of their families. They might write a letter to a grandparent or a relative in their country of origin. Students new to this country might write a letter poem to an American expressing their impressions of their new country.

❧ Letter to a Friend ❧

Come soon.

Everything is lusting

for light,

thrusting

up

up

splitting the earth,

opening flaring fading,

seed

into shoot

bud

into flower

nothing

beyond its hour.

Come soon.

The apple bloom has melted

like

spring snow.

→

FAVORITE POETRY LESSONS
Scholastic Professional Books, 1998

The lilac
changed the air,
surprising
every breath.

Low in the field
wild strawberries
fatten.

Come soon.

It's a matter of
life.

And death.

—Lilian Moore

❧ Scarecrow's Dream ❧

I think it's June—
crows landing in black waves.

Farmer arrives with his 22.
Stop, I say. And put away

that gun, I'll handle this.
Farmer shrugs, strides off.

For once I'm boss, and we're
a circle of friends. We discuss,

make deals: a little corn—
a little reticence. Come at night—

save your life. Peaceable
Kingdom I'm thinking when

I feel a step on my shoulder,
the first peck in my eye.

—Nina Nyhart

❧ Scarecrow's Dream ❧

READ THE POEM

In a sense, the persona poem is the opposite of the poem of address. In a persona poem, rather than addressing a person or thing, the writer *becomes* that subject and writes from its perspective. Nyhart's poem is one of my favorite persona poems, because it's so imaginative and creative, yet grounded in rich details.

DISCUSS THE POEM

As students and I talk about "Scarecrow's Dream," I tell them that I can imagine Nyhart driving by a field and seeing a scarecrow protecting the vegetable garden and wondering *What if*? I remind students that this question can be magical for writers. Nina Nyhart seems to have asked herself some interesting questions to get inside the scarecrow: What would it be like to be a scarecrow? What if it didn't like that job? What if it tried to make friends with crows? So, I tell students, one of the things you need to do to write a successful persona poem is to try to understand the essence of the subject and then imagine what this object might say. It might tell a story, like Nyhart's scarecrow, it might ask questions, or it might complain, like the cow in Alice Schertle's poem:

COW'S COMPLAINT

> How unkind to keep me here
> When, over there, the grass is greener
> Tender blades—so far, so near—
> How unkind to keep me here!
> Through this fence they make me peer
> At sweeter stems; what could be meaner?
> How unkind to keep me here
> When, over there, the grass in greener.

❧ IN THE POET'S WORDS... ❧

"I write first drafts with only the good angel on my shoulder, the voice that approves of everything I write. This voice doesn't ask questions like, 'Is this good? Is this a poem? Are you a poet?' I keep that voice at a distance, letting only the good angel whisper to me: 'Trust yourself.' You can't worry a poem into existence."

—Georgia Heard

WRITE THE POEM

In some ways, a poet is like a scientist. They both observe and report. The reports are different, of course—the scientist writes a prose report filled with numbers, graphs, a specialized vocabulary, whereas the poet writes a poem—but the process is similar: observe and report. Sometimes a poet will observe what is going on inside herself and write a poem about that. At other times she will observe something outside herself and write about that. But the observation part of the writing process is often crucial to writing a good poem, so kids need the time to observe and jot down some notes. These might consist of facts or physical observations or wonderings, all of which can become part of a poem.

POETRY LINKS

Social Studies: After studying a particular era in social studies, students can write a poem from the point of view of a person or object from that era—for example, the tea thrown into Boston Harbor, Paul Revere's horse, a slave working on the Pyramids, or the HMS *Titanic*. Pairs of students might write persona poems from opposite points of view—for example, a Union and a Confederate soldier.

Math: Have students try writing a poem from the point of view of a number. What would a zero feel like? What might it think? Or it might be interesting to write a poem as 1,000,000. Is it more fun being a million than a zero or any of those other numbers? Would a million look down its nose at "lesser" numbers?

Science: In her collection *Advice to a Frog*, Alice Schertle includes a couple of persona poems—from the point of view of a Galapagos turtle and a brown rat. You might wish to use these poems as models to demonstrate a skillful blend of history and natural science.

❧ Ten Little Likenesses ❧

1

The fly's buzz:
a radio tuned
where no station was.

2

Six
black
appleseeds
sleek
as beetles' backs

mark

where the eaten
apple's
left its tracks.

3

When the stoplight
drops
from red
to green
cars leap
like shot slung
from slingshot.

→

4
Like a bird
with salt on its tail,
the branch
freighted with snow
stands still.

5
River races
round its bend
like a pack
of black
cats,
dogs after them,
turning a corner.

6
It doesn't seem
to want to flow
downstream,
this full
moon like a yellow
beachball.

7
Open-billed
gulls
fighting
for fish heads
creak
like
rusted
gates.

8
From the phone wires
in quick
alarm
a flock
of crows
explodes.

9
At the sun's
target
earth
flings
spears:
white birches.

10
The river
flows down
to its delta
and sets sail
on the sea.

—X. J. Kennedy

FAVORITE POETRY LESSONS
Scholastic Professional Books, 1998

❧ Ten Little Likenesses ❧

READ THE POEM

X. J. Kennedy is one of the most talented poets writing for children. "Ten Little Likenesses" shows how a skilled poet can use metaphor and simile to create an image.

From the first section, this poem is rich in figurative language and can serve as a model for your students. Figurative language, like metaphors and similes, help the poet create an image in a poem. I even hate to use the word "image," because that connotes something visual, and an image in a poem will often appeal to other senses as well as sight. So images in poetry help us hear something or feel something or smell it.

DISCUSS THE POEM

When I talk with kids about this poem, I ask them to look at section 1 and note the metaphor—where one thing is something else—comparing a fly's buzz to the hum from a radio. I point out that a scientist would likely describe the sound of the fly in terms of frequency, modulation, volume. But the poet, hearing the same sound, writes a metaphor as his report. His comparison helps us hear. I say to kids, "Look at the last section of the poem for another metaphor—the poet comparing the river to a ship setting sail on the open sea. This metaphor helps us see the river, perhaps even feel it as it "sets sail on the sea."

I also highlight Kennedy's use of the simile, a comparison using "like" or "as." The appleseeds in part 2 are "sleek as beetles' backs." The moon in part 6 is "like a yellow beachball." And the gulls in the next section "creak like rusted gates." Note how these metaphors appeal to our senses, how they help us understand the image that Kennedy has created with his words.

When you use this poem as a model, point out that there is no beginning, middle, and end, as they might have come to expect. This poem is a collection of ten images— some involving animals or other wonders of nature—that was created to show similarities. Each section is a snapshot, if you will, or a sound bite.

❧ IN THE POET'S WORDS... ❧

"Poems are best delivered fast, sharp, smart and tellingly. They can help you realize something you could not understand before—they can illuminate the spirit with long forgotten beauties and uglies. Poetry is a true god-gift to humankind, also poetry is the opposite of hypocrisy."

—Gregory Corso

WRITE THE POEM

Ask your students to write one "likeness." When they write a good one, they can try for two. They might want to share their likenesses with you or their writing partners to see if they've created a clear image for the reader. If not, perhaps some constructive feedback might help them to tinker with the image. Remind them that they're doing more than simply describing something: They are writing "little likenesses" that create an image through the thoughtful use of metaphor and simile.

When students are ready to read their likenesses aloud, ask them to be on the lookout for likenesses that might be combined into a longer poem. For example, you might find that a number of your students wrote about things in the animal world or about things in their neighborhood. Or perhaps the likenesses involve sound or light or shape. Remember, there's no rule saying that a longer poem needs to have ten parts to it like Kennedy's. Any number will do fine. Here are a pair of "likenesses" written by seventh graders:

In the wind
leaves dart
like bats.
                    —Allie Taisey

The wind swishes
through the trees
like a friend
whispering
a secret.
                    —Justin Black

CRAFT CLOSE-UP: *Metaphor*

Life is a river.

The setting sun was an orange balloon.

A good metaphor goes beyond simple description. There is a certain equality implied in a clear metaphor: something is not merely *like* something else—something *is* something else. To write good metaphors, students need to have the time to observe and consider their subject. They need encouragement to see the object as something else—to describe it in a way that is more that just factual. You might ask your students questions that help them experience the object through their senses: Does it look like something else? If it has a sound, what does it sound like? Does that sound remind you of something else? Does the object have a function that might help the reader visualize it?

Writing poetry gets kids to see. As Thoreau said, "It's not what you look at, but what you see." And, I might add, how you see. It's important for young writers to look carefully and thoughtfully. But it is also important that they be able to go beyond the obvious, to write poems that give the writer a chance to make connections and give readers a chance to share how the poet sees the world. Metaphors and similes are tools that poets use to make such connections.

POETRY LINKS

Art: Send your students on a scavenger hunt—at school as well as at home—to search for some simple objects to sketch—for example, a key, a watch, a smooth stone, a feather, a bird's nest, nails. However, instead of sketching the objects, discuss each object in terms of its essential qualities, asking the students if it reminds them of something else. Such a discussion will give students the opportunity to start seeing objects in terms of other objects.

Social Studies: The scavenger hunt also works well in a social studies class. Have students bring in objects that are somehow related to their family history.

Worth Reading

Bruchac, Joseph. *The Earth Under Sky Bear's Feet: Native American Poems of the Land* (Philomel, 1995).

Carlson, Lori M., ed. *Cool Salsa: Bilingual Poems on Growing Up Latino in the United States* (Fawcett Books, 1995).

Chandra, Deborah. *Rich Lizard and Other Poems* (Farrar, 1993).

Graves, Donald. *Baseball, Snakes, and Summer Squash: Poems About Growing Up* (Boyds Mills, 1996).

Hopkins, Lee Bennett. *Been to Yesterdays: Poems of a Life* (Boyds Mills, 1994).

Hughes, Langston. *The Dream Keeper and Other Poems* (Knopf, 1994).

Janeczko, Paul B., ed. *The Place My Words Are Looking For* (Simon & Schuster, 1990).

—— *Poetry From A to Z: A Guide for Young Writers* (Simon & Schuster, 1994).

—— *That Sweet Diamond: Baseball Poems* (Atheneum, 1998).

Kuskin, Karla. *Near the Window Tree* (Harper, 1975).

Knudson, R. R., ed. *American Sports Poems* (Orchard, 1988).

Myers, Walter Dean. *Brown Angels* (Harper, 1993).

Nye, Naomi, ed. *The Tree Is Older Than You Are: A Bilingual Gathering of Poems & Stories From Mexico With Paintings by Mexican Artists* (Simon & Schuster, 1995).

Rylant, Cynthia. *Waiting to Waltz* (Bradbury Press, 1984).

Schertle, Alice. *Advice for a Frog* (Lothrop, 1995).

Soto, Gary. *Canto Familiar* (Harcourt, 1995).

Worth, Valerie. *All the Small Poems and Fourteen More* (Farrar, 1994).

FAVORITE POETRY LESSONS
Scholastic Professional Books, 1998

Publishing
Student Poems

Publishing is an important part of the writing process, but given that you probably have too much on your plate as a teacher, it wouldn't surprise me if the very thought of putting together a student anthology makes you sigh. Fortunately, there are a number of ways to publish student poetry without putting in long hours on each project.

Get Assistance

First look to the parents of your students for support. In my experience, there are always some who are happy to help you with a short-term project. Such volunteers could type student poems, run errands, pick up supplies and materials, photocopy poems, and so forth.

Contact a nearby high school, and see if you could "farm out" the typing of poems to a keyboarding class that is looking for practice. Perhaps the high school's art teacher or graphic arts teacher could arrange for a few responsible and talented students to work with younger students on their poetry projects.

Classroom Anthology

The easiest way to publish student poems is to type, photocopy, and staple them into booklets for each member of your class. If your students write one kind of poem at a time, you can then publish an anthology for clerihews, synonym poems, and so on. At the end of the term, you might want to consider having the students pick their best work for a general anthology.

You can also use a section of your classroom wall—or perhaps a space right outside your classroom door—to post poems in a sort of "wall anthology." Have kids create a colorful banner entitled something like Outta Sight Poems or Check Out These Poems, or From the Room 46 Poets.

Student Publications

If you have a school literary magazine, you have the perfect forum for the students to publish their poems. If you don't have such a magazine, you might give some thought to starting one. It *is* a great deal of work, but with a good student staff and some reliable parent volunteers, it could be a rewarding endeavor. You might want to see if a few teachers on your team or in your department would be interested in sharing the responsibility with you.

Your school newspaper should make it a point to publish student poetry. Granted, they will not have the room to publish many poems, but you might want to suggest that the newspaper carry a poetry column in every issue.

School Publications

A number of teachers I know publish a regular newsletter to keep parents abreast of what is happening in the classroom. These newsletters always include a student poem or two. If your district has a newsletter, you can lobby to make sure they include a student poem in each issue. Many districts would be more than happy to add a page to their newsletter if it would give them a chance to "show off" what their kids are doing.

Local Newspaper

Most small town and suburban newspapers set aside some space for news from the schools. They may be quite interested in occasionally including a student poem or two, especially if you can explain how such work would be a good change of pace from the usual straight news stories and informational articles.

National Publications and Contests

Although many publications that accept the work of students are legitimate, there are some that, under the guise of a "contest," publish student work in a thick book that they hope kids and school libraries will purchase. Beware of such deals. As a rule, I discourage young writers from submitting poetry to a magazine or contest that requires some sort of up-front payment or produces an expensive book for sale.

If you are looking for magazines that publish student work, you might consider *Children's Digest, Highlights for Children, Merlyn's Pen,* and *Creative Kids.* The single best source of information about publications and contests for young writers is *Market Guide for Young Writers* by Kathy Henderson (Betterway Publications, Inc., PO Box 219, Crozet, VA 22932). In addition to providing nuts and bolts information about publications and contests, Henderson also dishes out lots a savvy advice to any student (or concerned adult) interested in seeing his writing in print.

Other Possibilities

The suggestions that I've made so far do not involve a great deal of time or artistic talent. However, if you are interested in publishing student poems in a more elaborate and decorative fashion, I suggest you work with your kids to produce some wonderful posters, books, and cards.

There are a number of books that explore the role of publishing in the classroom. You might begin with *Classroom Publishing: A Practical Guide to Enhancing Student Literacy* by Laurie King and Dennis Stovall (Blue Heron Publishing, Inc., 24450 NW Hansen Road, Hillsboro, OR 97124), a book filled with exciting examples and practical how-to details. Paul Johnson has written two books for Heinemann that explain a holistic approach to developing children's writing and visual communication through what he calls "the book arts." *A Book of One's Own: Developing Literacy Through Making Books* is a comprehensive guide to book art. His second book, *Literacy Through the Book Arts*, shows how more than 50 book forms and variations can be produced with the bare necessities: paper, pen, and scissors.

In addition to Johnson's guides, there are a number of other worthwhile books about making books. The one I use the most—I can tell from all the brightly colored flags sticking out of my copy—is *75 Creative Ways to Publish Students' Writing* by Cherlyn Sunflower (Scholastic Professional Books). She covers all basic books, including accordion book, hand-sewn book, hinged book, pocket book, shape book, stitched book. In addition, she explains how to make banners, doorknob hangers, grocery bags, wanted posters, bookmarks, and neck tags. One of things I like so much about this book is that some of the publishing ideas—like the bookmark, doorknob hanger, neck tags—are well-suited for short poems.

There are two books that have wide application in middle school. *Multicultural Books to Make and Share* by Susan Kapuscinski Gaylord (Scholastic Professional Books) offers authentic book making ideas from Africa, the Americas, Asia, and Europe, as well as a historical overview of each area. *Making Books Across the Curriculum* by Natalie Walsh (Scholastic Professional Books) offers great ideas as well as literature and content area tie-ins.

Other books that offer suggestions and ideas for book making in the classroom are:

→ *Making Books* by Gillian Chapman and Pam Robson (Millbrook Press, 1992).

- *Making Shaped Books with Patterns* by Gillian Chapman and Pam Robson (Millbrook Press, 1995).

- *The Young Author's Do-It-Yourself Book* by Donna Guthrie, Nancy Bentley, and Katy Keck Arnsteen (Millbrook Press, 1994).

- *Book Craft* by Henry Pluckrose (Watts).

- *Making Cards* by Charlotte Stowell and Jim Robins (Larousse Kingfisher Chambers, 1995).

FAVORITE POETRY LESSONS
Scholastic Professional Books, 1998

Notes:

Notes: